COACHING SPECIAL SITUATIONS

BY THE EXPERTS

Edited by
Bob Murrey

COACHES CLINICS

ISBN: 1-58518-334-2

Library of Congress Catalog Card Number: 2001095167

Cover photo courtesy of Won-Up Productions
Cover design: Rebecca Gold
Book layout: Jennifer Bokelmann

Coaches Choice
P.O. Box 1828
Monterey, CA 93942
http://www.coacheschoiceweb.com

Additional information on either the USA Coaches Clinic schedule or the USA Coaches library can be obtained by either calling 1-800-COACH-13 or faxing 1-314-991-1929.

Throughout this book, the masculine shall be deemed to include the feminine and vice versa.

CONTENTS

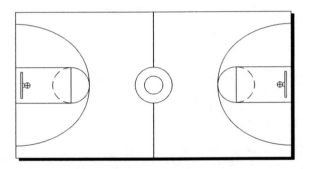

PLAYERS

(5) Centers

(3, 4) Forwards

(1, 2) Guards

◯ = Offense

X = Defense

⊙ = Player with the Ball

– – → = Direct Pass

——⊣ = Screen

∿∿→ = Dribble

——→ = Cut of Player with or without the Ball

⊞⊞⊞⊞→ = Shot

CHAPTER 1

TRANSITION BASKETBALL

JOAN BONVICINI

I'm here to talk about transition basketball and some things that I do to organize our program. One of the first things I do is to set up *goals* for the team. I have *10 offensive and 10 defensive* goals. You will have to adjust them to the level of your program.

OFFENSIVE TEAM GOALS PER GAME

- Shoot 51% as a team from the floor.
- Take a minimum of 70 shots.
- Shoot 70% from the free-throw line.
- Shoot 20 free throws.
- Get eight fast-break baskets.
- Get 12 offensive rebounds.
- Get 20 assists.
- Commit no more than 17 turnovers.
- Have no 30-second violations.
- Score at least 85 points.

DEFENSIVE TEAM GOALS PER GAME

- Hold opponents to 42% field goal percentage.
- Allow a maximum of 60 shots.
- Allow a maximum of 15 free throws.
- Out rebound the opponent by five or more.
- Allow a maximum of 12 assists.
- Force a minimum of 20 turnovers.
- Force one 30-second violation.
- Take two charges.
- Get at least eight steals.
- Allow no more than 70 points.

I give these goals to each player, and they put them in their notebook.

Obviously, if we are going to play a tough opponent, I will adjust them before the game. We will put these on the board at halftime. Your *goals must be realistic* so you must adjust them to fit your level, but maybe, as the season progresses, you can increase them. It makes a big difference if you put them down as *team goals* as opposed to individual goals.

Something else I did. Coach John Wooden had a Pyramid of Success. I made a little pyramid, too. At the bottom, I put all of our nonconference opponents, and I listed them. Then, at the next level, I listed all the conference opponents. Above that, I put in the conference tournament and each level of the playoffs. The players really liked that. They would put up the pyramid in the locker room before a game, with the goals listed. This also went into the notebooks. Before the season starts, I make a chart of what I must cover for the season, and then break it down into week by week prior to the first game. Because of the shortening of our preseason, I tried to put in too much too soon. I learned a good lesson. We needed more fundamental teaching. So, keep it simple and then build on it as the season progresses.

Before the season starts, I put out a master plan and discuss it with the staff. This includes all the things I want to teach for that particular year. I list conditioning and fundamentals. Under fundamentals, I list *individual offense and individual defense.* Then, I list the team offenses and defenses, transition game, jump-ball offense, free-throw situations, out-of-bounds plays, and presses. Then, these must be put in week-by-week prior to the start of the season.

My main topic is *transition.* I always considered myself a fast-break coach; I was averaging about 80 points per game. When I put this in, we went to 90 points per game. What happened is that our pace is very difficult to defend. It's not like Westhead when he was at Loyola–Marymount. We worked at defense, too. Let's start at the beginning, the way I do it.

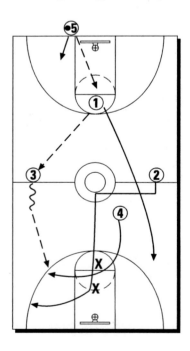

DIAGRAM 1-1.

5 takes it out-of-bounds. 5 must get the ball out of the net before it hits the floor, steps out-of-bounds and throws the baseball pass. 1, the point guard, starts about the free-throw line extended. The further you start the guard from the baseline, the faster she will get down the floor.

1 is in the middle of the court. 1 will make one or two dribbles and make a chest pass on the run to either 2 or 3. You don't necessarily use your best ball handler here because she is only going to make one or two dribbles. But, she must be able to make the chest pass on the run. 2 is on the left side of the court; 3 on the right. No matter where they are when the ball

is shot, *2 will always go on the left, 3 on the right.* They must be able to catch the ball on the run and should be good perimeter shooters. 4 is generally the big forward. As soon as the basket is made, 4 runs the middle of the floor and goes mid-post ballside. 4 will then reverse pivot.

DIAGRAM 1-2.

3 has the ball; 4 is on the block; 2 is in the corner; 1 went opposite and is spotting up on the weakside. 5 is the trailer. 3 can pass to 2 or 4, but in this case, reverses to 5 who passes to 1. 4 flashes toward 5 as 5 has the ball. 5 can shoot the three-pointer as an option. After 5 passes to 1, 5 cuts to the block. 4 fills the high post.

DIAGRAM 1-3.

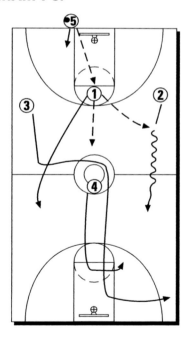

5 inbounds to 1 and 1 passes ahead to 2. 4 goes down the middle and posts up on the strongside block. 1 goes away. 3 cuts to the middle. 2 dribbles down the side. When 3 fills the middle, the cut to the ball must be a *direct cut.* Do not cut on a *diagonal.* Make an "L" cut. 3 then goes to the corner. If 2 and 3 can't handle the ball, have 1 dribble down the middle until 2 and 3 spot up.

DIAGRAM 1-4.

3 is in the corner and you have a triangle with 2, 3, and 4. 2 passes to 3 in the corner. The defense must make a decision to guard either the corner or the post. 2 interchanges with 1. This keeps 2's defender from double-teaming in the corner.

DIAGRAM 1-5.

3 passes to 1 to 5 to 2. 5 cuts to the low post; 4 comes high. *The person on the block is the number one option.* We want her to get the ball as often as possible. That's why the strong reverse pivot. Some years, I made 4 and 5 interchangeable.

DIAGRAM 1-6.

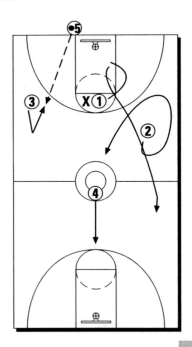

Let's say that 1 is guarded. 1 runs a *circle route* to try to get the ball. 3 and 2 have started to run, but it is important that they are not more than 15 feet from 1. When 2 and 3 see 1 being guarded, they come back. Suppose this time 5 passes to 3. 3 takes the ball on the dribble; 1 goes opposite; 2 goes middle. 4 posts up on the strongside block. If 5 has a strong arm, she can pass the ball to half-court to 2 or 3. When you run this system, your opponents will be so conscious of this that instead of sending four players to the offensive boards, they will send three.

DIAGRAM 1-7. SKIP-PASSES

3 has the ball; 2 runs the turnout; 4 is on the block. Instead of passing to 5, 3 skip-passes to 1. If 1 has the three-point shot, she shoots it. 5 cuts to the block; 4 flashes high. 3 fills at the point. You must teach your team when this *transition ends* and when we start our *regular offense. It ends when we have a reversal and get nothing out of it.*

DIAGRAM 1-8.

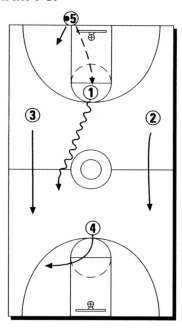

Assume that 2 and 3 are not open. 1 declares a side. 2 will remain opposite. 5 will come down and set a screen.

DIAGRAM 1-9.

1 keeps the dribble. 5 sets a screen for 1 near the top of the circle and goes to the block. 1 could have the jump shot, or 1 can pass to 2 for the shot. 5 can also step back and get the pass back from 1. 4 then goes to the high post.

DIAGRAM 1-10.

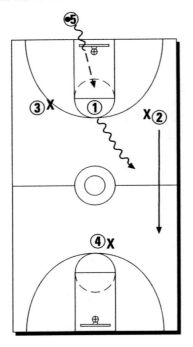

This is how opponents try to stop this. They allow the point guard to get the ball and they defend 2, 3 and 4. It is very important that 1 declares a side and stays on that side. This makes the screen by 5 very important.

DIAGRAM 1-11.

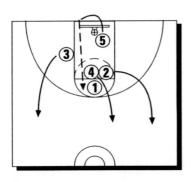

This is the way we practice it, starting on the first day of practice. Prior to going out on the floor, I tell each person her position. Then I diagram and go through the simple options in the beginning. Then we will walk through it, stressing the importance of how 5 takes the ball out of the net. The point guard must start in the middle of the court. If 1 goes on the side, she takes away the option to the wing. I do 5-on-0 every single day. All five players are in the key. 5 puts the ball in the basket and we break. I will give them options—no defense, rebound all missed shots.

DIAGRAM 1-12.

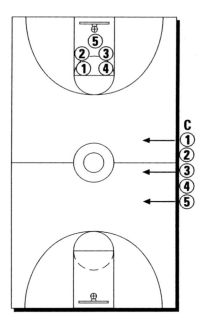

Then we practice "5 on." We have a coach near mid-court with five defensive players. She will send out three players, or four players or all five. They could be trapping or challenging the point guard. We spend 10 to 15 minutes a day on this. *When don't we run transition?* On a dead ball, if it's a crucial part of the game, or at the end of a close game.

DIAGRAM 1-13.

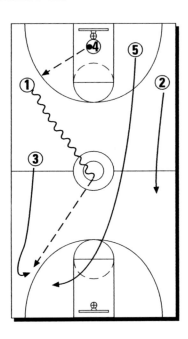

After a missed basket, we do the same thing. Suppose 4 rebounds and outlets to 1. 1 fills the middle and 2 and 3 run wide. The player who didn't get the rebound, player 5, goes to the block on the ballside. I like the fast break. It's fun to play and fun to watch. More kids are going to play, and they must be in shape.

DIAGRAM 1-14.

If you are being pressed and the ball is inbounded to 3, 1 goes away and 2 replaces.

DIAGRAM 1-15.

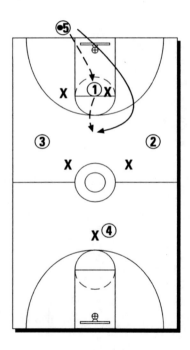

DIAGRAM 1-16.

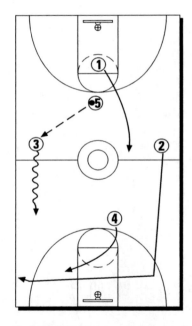

With this system, people are afraid to press you. But let's say that they do press with a 2-2-1. 1 must come up to get the ball. 1 gets trapped. 5 does a *semicircle*, and I promise you, 5 will be open for the pass from 1. 2 and 3 are now open for the pass from 5. I don't let 5 dribble. 5 catches, jump stops, and passes to 2 or 3.

3 dribbles down; 2 does a *turnout*; 4 is on the block, and we are in the offense. I don't believe that you can run an offense like ours and then sit in a 2-3 zone on defense. I have always liked to *switch* defenses.

CHAPTER 2

SPECIAL SITUATIONS

HUBIE BROWN

Recently, I did a Final Four European Clinic in Spain. Everything is done on the basketball court itself. Twenty countries and 750 coaches were represented there. When I finished my portion of the clinic, I was asked to do an interview for the best European basketball magazine. At the end of the interview, I asked the reporter how the clinic went. He stated that it was a good clinic, but that maybe I spoke over the coaches heads. Because I demonstrated what I discussed, he felt some things may actually have sunk in. Well, that is what I am going to do here. I am going to give you an awful lot of information and food for thought. I hope some of what you are about to hear will sink in and get you to think about what you are doing as a coach. Let's get started.

What do you say in your *time-out*? Syracuse vs. Arkansas, a man dives on the floor to recover the ball for Syracuse and seal the game. A Syracuse player calls time-out; Syracuse has none left. The same thing occurred in the Michigan vs. North Carolina Final Four championship game several years ago. In a Big East game between St. Johns and Georgetown and in an ACC game between Florida State and North Carolina, the same thing happens. A technical foul was called in all four games because a team called a sixth time-out and in all four cases, the team making the time-out call loses the game.

I suffered the same *humiliation* playing for Niagara in 1954. On national television, I made a time-out call when we had none left. I know the hurt and humiliation the players experienced in these other situations. Probably the greatest question ever asked of me was in a clinic I was doing in Ireland. A little, old nun attended this clinic and during the question and answer session, she raised her hand and stated, "Forget about all the X's and O's, what do you tell the laddies and lassies when you call a time-out?"

In a defensive huddle we cover the following:

- Who is the other team's best offensive rebounder? Forget what they run, if they shoot and miss, who do we want to make sure to keep off the boards? We have taught all our players to go to the baseline, under the basket and back out on the off-side. We want to make sure we don't let this happen to us.

- Who do we foul if necessary?

- Who are the three-point shooters for the opponent?
- Are we in the penalty? Can we foul?
- We then discuss their pet play. We used a magnetic board to show this. I am a firm believer that if our players see it, they'll remember it. Let me give you several situations that occurred to me and convinced me that a magnetic board was the way to go. In 1964, Duke is playing in the Final Four and Vic Bubas calls a time-out. On his knees he is chalking a play on the floor for the team to run. As he steps back from the play to explain it to the team, the senior team manager leans over the huddle to take a look at it and spills water onto the floor sending the play running down the sideline.

  Here's another story that happened to me when I was an assistant coach at Milwaukee and we were playing the New York Knicks. We broke the huddle and as the team was leaving, Kareem turns to me and says, "Hubie, who's the shooter?" Oscar Robertson jumps in and says, "Who cares who the shooter is, who's taking the ball out-of-bounds?" I take a look at the play that was drawn on a legal pad and all I can make out is a bunch of lines running all over the page. This is why we used a magnetic board to cover our plays. We put the numbers 1, 2, 3, 4 and 5 on one set of magnets and F, F, C, G, and G on the other set. The players can relate to these markers, and it is easier for them to visualize without drawing up a bunch of lines that run together or putting a play on the floor that could be wiped out.

- The last thing we cover is the number of time-outs we have remaining. What is your last instruction to your team before leaving the huddle? Did you tell them? If not, you're leaving yourself open for severe criticism, or if the athletic director is out to get you, a possibility of being fired.

In an offensive huddle we cover the following:

- The play we want to run.
- Time-outs we have remaining.
- Are we shooting the penalty?
- What defense we will run if we make the shot or if we miss the shot?

Always *change defenses* if a team calls time-out and has to go the length of the floor. *When the ball goes through the hole, don't call a time-out,* don't give the other team a chance to change their defense. Get the ball out-of-bounds, get it back in, run your sideline break and when you get the ball to the 28' mark on your offensive end, run your secondary break or if you don't have anything, then call your time-out.

When you're shooting a free-throw with 1, 2, or 3 seconds left in the game and you're up by 2 or 3, do you pull your team off the lane and send them back to the offensive end? If you're going to send all your players back, make sure you're up by four or that you have some type of play to deal with this. Let me offer you a better solution.

DIAGRAM 2-1.

Place your players on the foul line and designate who will cover whom. Stress to your players that they are to stay between the opponent's basket and the ball and not to foul.

How do you *communicate* with your team when you're going to the basket away from your bench? We have our post players on the box and looking at the clock so they can make the call of when we start our play. They can also see the bench so they can state what play we're going to be running.

What do you do when you're tied and there are 10-12 seconds left? We start our play with six or seven seconds left to go. We do this because it gives us a chance to shoot and get the offensive rebound.

When do you go when you're tied? If you are holding until the end, you must know the tremendous pressure you're putting on your player to make the shot.

Are the rims loose or tight where you're playing? If the rims are tight, you must rebound further out because the ball will come out long. Your guards have to be told to get back to the foul line, and the inside players must block out outside the dotted circle in the foul lane.

Always press a pressing team. I have been involved in basketball since 1959, and I have, as of yet, to see a pressing team that handles the press well. In the Arkansas vs. Kentucky game this year, we saw the two best teams, talent-wise, in America playing. These were supposedly two well-coached teams who love to press and *work against it everyday*, yet at halftime they had 20 turnovers apiece.

When teaching the press, never mention the word steal, talk *position* of the floor to your players. Stress to them that when pressing, they must rotate back to the basket and stop all layups. Nothing can destroy a pressing team's morale more than to give up easy layups. If you don't have a shot blocker to put deep on your press, teach your players to rotate into the lane and take the charge.

How do you stop the clock with no time-outs left? We have several options ready to go:

- Designate the player who is going to lose his contact.
- Water on the floor—designate a player to throw a little water on the floor and then have your bench yell: "There's water on the floor." The officials will stop the clock every time. Make sure, however, that you are nowhere near the spot when it occurs.

- Fake an injury. Make sure, however, that the player you designate to fake the injury isn't your star player because he has to come out of the game due to an injury.
- Will you take the sixth time-out and accept a technical? Do you have the courage to do this?

What is your *strategy* when you are down five? I go for the two points first. I don't want to shoot the three first. I believe this because invariably when you go for the three, you'll miss, you'll foul, and you'll need two 3's instead of one. I believe you get the two, get into your *denial press*, and take your chances.

I want to share four plays that I know work. The situation is three down, shooting two free- throws.

DIAGRAM 2-2.

You make the first free-throw and now you're two down. On the second shot, 2 steps to the dotted circle, not to the basket. 1 moves to the other side of the basket. If 2 can't get the ball, he looks to tap the ball to free-throw shooter 3, who has moved to the side of the free-throw line. If 1 rebounds the ball, he takes it right back up and sticks it in.

DIAGRAM 2-3.

Another option in this situation is for 4 to loop to the baseline and to the basket. The free-throw shooter misses to 4's side, 4 rebounds, scores, tie game, and over-time.

DIAGRAM 2-4.

A third option — I saw this done in a high school regional game — is to miss the second shot, loop 4 to the baseline, 5 back-screens the man who is blocking him out, 4 lobs the rebound out to 3, who has stepped behind 5's screen, and 3 shoots the three.

DIAGRAM 2-5.

This is a play that Philadelphia ran against me years ago. Two seconds to go. Dawkins and McGinnis were on the inside boxes. Jones and Erving were lined up on the top of the circle behind the shooter who was Doug Collins. Collins shot the ball to hit it off the front of the rim. Dawkins and McGinnis, on the shot, ran a curl to the outside. Jones broke straight down the lane to occupy one of the defensive players on the top of the lane. Erving faked a step in and then rolled to the outside and moved untouched to the basket.

When do you practice your game situations? Do you get to the first game of the season and you haven't practiced any? We practiced our game situation drills three times a week for five minutes.

Never run a screen and roll from the wing with a player on the post. Why? Because the roll player has nowhere to go. The Boston Celtics handled the screen and roll from the wing by tapping the roller.

DIAGRAM 2-6.

If you're going to screen and roll, get *good spacing* on the weakside. When you teach the screen and roll, make sure to tell your dribbler he must come off the screen, take two dribbles, not one dribble, and on the second dribble, turn the corner.

Next, I want to talk about the cardinal rules of basketball, *post play*.

How do you feed the post? We have two things that we teach. One, you *never* feed the post while above the foul line. If you do this, you allow the defensive man the opportunity to get to the ball. The post should run to the first marker above the box. This marker should split your post in half. Why? Because now you can turn to the middle and you can turn to the baseline and have the bank shot. When you post up, have the opposite post vacant. Why? Because you can't throw the lob. The opposite side post is there to stop the lob or the power move. When you teach your players to post up, have them bring their hands up with their thumbs pointing to their ears and have them sit on the defender's thigh. This takes the defender out of the play because it *neutralizes* his ability to move.

What is this technique we teach to *equalize* a good post player in good post position? We teach the defender to place his back knee in the back of the post player's knee and apply pressure to the knee. This forces the offensive player's knee to collapse and makes it hard to catch the ball. Good players who have attended good camps have been taught this technique.

What do we do to *counteract* the defense taking away the post's spot? We use a technique that Bernard King was good at executing. The offensive player comes down and moves into the defender with his hands up; this eliminates the chance of a pushing call and makes the official focus his attention on my hands. I also place my outside leg between the defender's legs, pivot to the ball, and sit on the defender's leg with a wide base. Even if the defense moves his leg away, the offense will still stand because of good balance.

Never pass to a post-up person until he *calls* for the ball. How many times does your guard pass to the post, who is still fighting for position, and you lose the ball? Guards don't pass to the post until he/she calls for the ball, and then the guard must pass to the hand he/she calls for it with.

How many people do you send to rebound a shot? How many people do you send back on the shot? We never send a guard to the offensive boards. If the center shoots, the two forwards and center go to the boards. If the forward shoots a jump shot outside the lane, we send the center and other forward to the board, and the forward who shot and the two guards back. Why? Because the ball is going to rebound long, and we want to stop the break that will materialize quicker. If the forward puts the ball on the floor and shoots in the lane, we send both forwards and the center to the board. Why? Because if I shoot in the paint, it will be a short rebound and I continue my momentum toward the board. If a guard drives to the basket and shoots the layup, he still gets back. This can be done. If the guard says he can't get back, you bring him out and sit him down. This will motivate the player to do it if he wants to play. We teach this rebounding concept everyday when we run our skeleton offensive drill.

Are your out-of-bounds plays designed to work against both man and zone defenses? Do you try to score on your zone out-of-bound's plays? I believe the out-of-bound's plays you run must be capable of producing a score no matter the defense you're facing.

DIAGRAM 2-7.

In running your out-of-bound's plays, I feel you must cover the four areas I've designated with dark circles. I believe you also need no more than three seconds to get the ball inbounds. I'm going to share with you some out-of-bound's plays that have been good to me.

DIAGRAM 2-8.

We line up in a box. We are going to screen a screener. 1 screens for 2, who comes off the screen and to the outside top spot. 4 screens the screener 1, and 1 comes down the lane. 3 lobs to 1 for the dunk. 5 cuts off the lane and to the outside baseline spot. 4 is open to come down the lane for the inbound pass if 1 hasn't gotten open.

DIAGRAM 2-9.

Another out-of-bounds play we have found to be quite successful is set up with 3 & 5 stacking on the lane, 4 lined up on the ballside elbow, and 2 in the baseline corner away from the ball. 3 has both hands on 5's hip. 5 dropsteps to the ball; 3 steps out toward the ballside corner. 4 comes down the lane and screens for 2. 2 cuts outside 4's screen and high. 4 continues down the lane to screen for 1, the inbounder. 1 passes to 3 and comes off 4's screen. 3 passes to 2, who can shoot the three or look to pass to 1 coming off 4's screen for the three.

DIAGRAM 2-10.

If they attempt to put a defender on the inside and outside of our stack, 5 would cut out and 3 would come down the lane behind 5 for the quick pass in.

DIAGRAM 2-11.

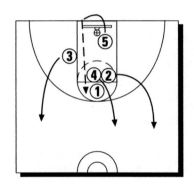

A final out-of-bounds play that has worked for us is something we called "X." 5 cuts to the corner; 3 steps to the right side of the lane. 4 screens down for 2, who comes high off the screen and to the ballside guard position.

DIAGRAM 2-12.

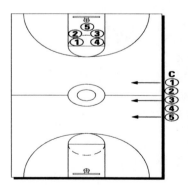

1 passes to 5 and steps inbounds right under the basket. 5 reverses the ball to 2. 4 comes down and sets a screen for 1. 5, after passing to 2, comes inside and sets a second screen for 1. 1 comes off the staggered-screens to the corner looking for the open three.

DIAGRAM 2-13.

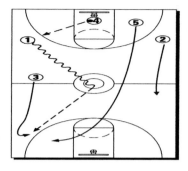

3 sets a screen for 4, and 2 can hit 4 for the open jumper if 1 is not open in the corner.

Do you have any set plays from a sideline out-of-bound's situation? Here are several I think you'll find to be to your liking.

DIAGRAM 2-14.

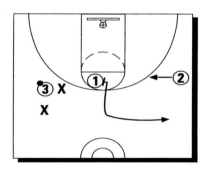

4 and 5 set up at the low-post positions. 3 sets up at the foul line extended, and 2 lines up two to three steps above 3. 4 will cut to the ballside corner. 2 comes down and screens for 3.

DIAGRAM 2-15.

After screening for 3, 2 continues down the lane and screens for 5. If the defense attempts to switch on 2's screen for 5, he 2. slips the screen, cuts to the ballside box, and looks to catch the pass and score.

DIAGRAM 2-16.

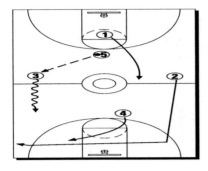

Another play we'll run sees us stack 4 and 5 on the foul lane and have 3 line up directly under the basket. 2 lines up on the foul line. 2 starts by screening down for 3, who cuts off the screen and to the point. 4 comes off the stack and looks to head hunt in the lane for 2. 5 drops toward the baseline and looks to set a second screen for 2. 2 comes off the screen and to the ballside corner.

DIAGRAM 2-17.

5, after screening for 2, comes to the ball. 1 passes to 5, who must pivot to the inside. 3 breaks to the rim on the pass to 5. 4 moves to the weakside "junction." 5 can hit 4 or 3, but what we really want is for 5 to turn, swing, one bounce to the basket, and score.

DIAGRAM 2-18.

A variation that the Detroit Pistons ran to this out-of-bounds play was to pass to 5 coming to the ball, have 2 come off the baseline to screen for 1, 1 cut to the corner, and 5 hit 1 in the corner for the open three.

DIAGRAM 2-19.

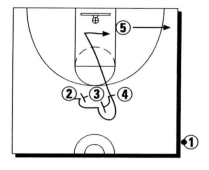

The final sideline out-of-bound's play I'll share with you starts with 2, 3, and 4 stacked at the top of the circle and 5 on the ballside block. 2 cuts off screens by 3 & 4 and goes down the lane to replace 5 who has cut to the ballside corner.

DIAGRAM 2-20.

1 passes to 4 and gets a return pass from 4. On the pass to 4, 3 moves down the lane and looks to set a screen for 2. On the pass back, 1 and 4 run a screen and roll. 1 now has an open shot, drive to the basket, or can dump the ball to 2 coming off 3's screen for the open shot.

The last thing I want to share with you is a great offense against a box-and-one or a triangle-and-two. I saw the Brazilian women's team run this, and they ran it to perfection. They are a sound, high-powered team. They run this offense for their great player, Hortensia. Hortensia only scored 32 points against the United States women's team running this offense.

When you're playing against a box-and-one or triangle-and-two, always put the player being singled out on the baseline. They took their center and their small forward and put them on the one side of the baseline with Hortensia. The best woman ballhandler in the world is at the point. The fifth player is at the wing on the side away from the triple. The option they now have is:

DIAGRAM 2-21.

Hortensia (H) can fake in toward the baseline, the defense will attempt to beat her to the spot, 1 will cut off the top of the screen. If the defense tries to follow her over the top of the screen, she is open for a pass inside and a short jumper.

DIAGRAM 2-22.

If the defense tries to go around the back of the screen, H steps back toward the sideline and looks for the pass and shot on the baseline.

DIAGRAM 2-23.

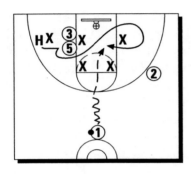

Hortensia (H) could now cut off the top of the doublescreen, cut through the zone and if the defense follows her, she would run a curl around the defensive forward on the opposite side.

DIAGRAM 2-24.

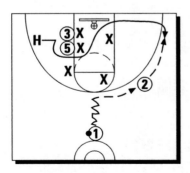

Hortensia (H) could cut off the top of the double, cut through the zone and if they use the other zone members to play this cut, she would bump the offside forward and float to the corner for a pass from the point to the wing to her in the corner. What can the rest of the offensive players do to take advantage of this defense?

DIAGRAM 2-25.

As the ball was passed to the offside wing and Hortensia cut to the corner, they would reverse the ball back to the point, forcing the defensive guard to play man-to-man. The center now picks the back of the defense, and the forward steps off the screen for an open 8' jumper.

DIAGRAM 2-26.

Now what if the offside forward fights over the top of the zone and comes out hard on the forward? The center, after setting the screen, opens up and pins the forward coming back from the ballside. The forward now passes it into the center for an easy layup.

DIAGRAM 2-27.

Another option is: as the forward fights over the top of the screen, the point guard fakes a pass to the forward and hits the center in the middle of the lane before the offside forward can get back.

CHAPTER 3

LATE GAME SITUATIONS

JOHN CALIPARI

We have three rules we now have to be aware of in late-game situations:

- 35 seconds instead of 45
- Clock stops after every made basket during the last minute of play
- No five-second count.

I don't believe in calling time-outs during the last minutes of the game. We're at Syracuse and I see the game slipping away, so I call time-out. I cover what to do if they go man and one of my players asks what to do if they go zone. So we cover this also. We go back out and Syracuse is in a zone. All my players know what to do except one, who wasn't paying attention during the time-out. Instead of taking a time-out in a late game situation to cover something that someone might forget, we cover all these situations in practice so we don't need to call time-outs. Here's a situation: three point game, you're behind with 40 seconds to go, what is your team thinking about if on offense? We take the best shot available and look to close the gap. This will put us in a position to win.

Here's another one: down five with 45 seconds to a minute to go, what will you do? We'll shoot a two. If down six, we might shoot a three, but if we shoot, miss, rebound it, we put it back in. Now we're down four and are back in the game. Why settle for a jump shot at the end of the game when the other team's coach is telling his players not to foul? Thus, when you drive the basket for the layup, the last thing the opponent wants to do is foul.

Here are some late game situations we use at UMass:

DIAGRAM 3-1. WINNER

We use this when we have 12 seconds or more left to play. We set 2 and 3 on the blocks while 4 and 5 line up at the top of the circle. 1 brings the ball down and dribbles off a screen set by 4 or 5. In this example, it will be 4. As 1 comes off the screen, he looks for a shot.

DIAGRAM 3-2.

2 and 3 set a *double back-screen* for 5. 5 cuts to the *box* on the ballside. 3 rolls back to the ball after screening for 5. 2 back-screens for 4 and *pops* out.

DIAGRAM 3-3.

4 cuts off the back-screen looking for a *pass* from 1. If 1 passes to 5, we have 2 back-screen for 4 and 5 looks to 4 on the *back cut.* If 1 passes to 2, we tell 2 to look for 4 and if 4 isn't open, to shoot the ball because we have our best rebounders 3, 4, and 5 near the basket.

We like to make a last second play off a *dribble entry play.* Why? Because if you have to do it with a pass and if the pass isn't there, your whole future is in trouble. Have you ever thought about a last second *defensive situation play?* Here is one to consider:

DIAGRAM 3-4.

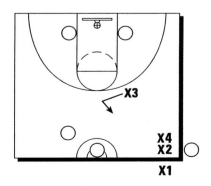

We place two of our biggest players on the inbounder. X2 doesn't allow the ball inbound on the sideline. X1 doesn't allow the ball inbound on the back cut. X3, your best athlete, looks for the pass to the middle.

DIAGRAM 3-5.

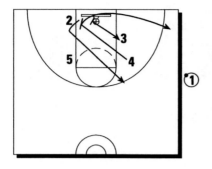

A late-game play we use from the sideline is as follows. 1 takes the ball out of bounds. 2, 3, 4, and 5 set up on the lane in a box. 4 screens for 2 breaking to the ball. 3 sets a screen for 4, who cuts to the corner off the screen. 3 *rolls back* to the ball after setting the screen.

DIAGRAM 3-6.

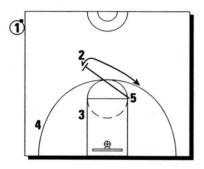

If 3 or 4 aren't open, 5 sets a *back-screen* for 2 and we go over the top to 2.

DIAGRAM 3-7.

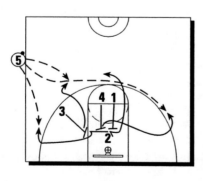

Another play we use to get a three-point shot late in the game is shown in Diagram 3-7. 1, 2, 3, and 4 are our best three-point shooters. 1 and 4 set up on the foul line. 2 sets up in the lane with 3 lining up on the wing of the ballside. 5 takes the ball out-of-bounds. 1 and 4 move down the lane to set a double-screen for 2. 3 moves to the *box* on the ballside. After setting the screen for 2, 4 cuts to the *corner off the ball* and 1 cuts off a screen set by 3 to the *corner on the ballside.* After setting the screen for 1, 3 breaks back to the ball. All three players 1, 3, and 4 make sure they are behind the three-point line. 5 can throw over the top to 4, to 1 breaking to the corner, or to 3 *stepping back* to the ball. If 2 is the player open for the pass from 5, you're in trouble.

DIAGRAM 3-8.

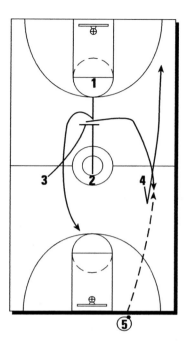

A full-court play we use in a late game situation is shown in Diagram 3-8. 5 takes the ball out of bounds; 2, 3, and 4 set up at the half-court line; and 1 sets up at the foul line at the offensive end. When 5 gets the ball, 4 *fakes* a cut to the ball and *breaks deep*. 4 gives the fake that he is going to get the long pass. 2 and 3 set a *double back-screen* for 1. 1 breaks off the screen to the ball. 3, after setting the screen, runs to the area vacated by 4. 5 passes to 3 and then we call time-out. We now can set up our half-court sideline play.

CHAPTER 4

LAST-SECOND SHOTS

NANCY FAHEY

The reasons coaches have so many questions about last-second shots is because of the variables involved. It makes a difference if there are 10 seconds left or if there are five seconds left. Who's in the game? How many time-outs do you have? Are you home or away? How are the officials calling the game? So there is *NO* one single formula that you should use. The thing that gives you the advantage is that you *prepare* as much as you possibly can to minimize the impact of those variables. Don't assume that it will happen unless you practice it.

We cover some type of situation every day in practice. When you go into a game, you must know how your players are going to react, and you must know what play you are going to use in each situation. Your team knows them. You know who wants the ball in the *pressure situation* and who does not. So, you know that if the play didn't work, at least your team was prepared. That is some comfort.

THINGS YOU CAN DO IN PRACTICE:

- Use the clock. Simulate game situations, put the score on the board. Many players have no concept as to how long five seconds is. The inbounders must know how long five seconds is and that they can call a time-out only in the first three seconds.

- Use various combinations of players in practice. Don't pick your best five players every time. What happens in the game when one of these players has fouled out?

- Create a competitive situation through rewards and ramifications. Don't always make yourself the bad guy. Make the players decide on the penalty. I will ask, "Winners, what are you going to do?" They might say that they will get water. I then ask, "Losers, what are you going to do?" They will decide on something easy. Then I'll ask, "Is that all the confidence you have in yourself?" Now they will decide and make it more meaningful. They will learn to make themselves better.

- Make it tougher for the offense by adding an extra defensive player.

- Practice time-outs. Don't use three minutes for a time-out during practice. Limit yourself to sixty seconds. Make sure the team understands how long 60 seconds is. I have my point guard sitting directly in front of me. My 2 and

3 players are next to the guard, and 4 and 5 are on the outside. We practice 60 seconds, and don't give yourself unlimited time-outs during practice.

- Educate your team as to when they have the green light to call a time-out. My players do not have the option to call a time-out unless I tell them. They do not have the green light in the first half. Ideally, I want to have three time-outs remaining with five minutes left in the game. Then, I will allow the team to use one of them. You must tell your team how many time-outs you have remaining.

- Your team must know the team foul situation. Do you have a foul to give? If you are not in the bonus, foul the other team when they are attacking the basket. Now they will have to take the ball out-of-bounds and re-set. It will take time off the clock.

- Teach them how to foul. You don't want to get the intentional foul and you don't want to hurt anyone. Go for the ball.

- If you have a shot clock, make sure that you know the shot clock rules.

- Sometimes in practice we set up a situation and a player will call time-out. We give a technical foul and tell that player we were over the limit. She didn't ask how many time-outs we had left.

GAME PREPARATION

- If you are going to call time-out to set up a play, make sure you know where you want the ball to be, under the basket or on the sideline. Pre-determine this and then make sure the official agrees with you as to where the ball is put in play.

- Have your assistant coach know ahead of time who you are going to foul. Have as many as five listed, with their free-throw percentages.

- When it gets under two minutes, do not hesitate to sub from offense to defense.

- If you have coached against a coach over the years, you should know the tendencies of that coach. Is this coach always going to play player-to-player, or will he switch to a zone? When you call a time-out, you give that coach a chance to do things to you.

- Prepare a last-second book on the sideline. Have the plays drawn up, open the book and show them the play. This is the same book I bring to practice. Have it drawn for both sides and make sure that you show them the play exactly how it is going to be facing. Don't show them the play going the opposite direction.

DEFENSIVE STRATEGIES

- *Zones:* If you are getting beat on the inside, you may want to consider a zone. Another advantage is that there is less chance to foul. It also helps you to stop the screens. Most teams, during the last seconds of a game, are probably developing a play to be used against a player-to-player defense.

The disadvantage of using a zone is that it is difficult to defend the outside shot.

- *Player-to-Player:* If they don't have a player who can just "shoot down the court," I think it will slow the player down. Make them zig-zag. It is a good idea to go player-to-player if they have a star. If they are going to one player, this will help. We will switch on all perimeter screens if the other team needs to make a three-point shot. Be sure you don't foul the three-point shooter.

- *Do you put someone on the ball on the baseline defense?* If it's under three or four seconds and if the gym has a small area around the playing court, put someone on the ball. I want to eliminate the flat inbounds pass. I want to make the other team arc the pass. If there are 10 seconds, I will take the player off the ball. If you have someone on the ball, watch out for back-screens, especially if there are less than two seconds.

DIAGRAM 4-1.

We face our player away from the endline, or away from the sideline as the official hands the player the ball. She watches who breaks free and double-teams that person. We don't want the ball to get inbounds, so turn to the defense and try to double up.

OFFENSIVE STRATEGIES

If there are 10 seconds left in the game and you are behind, do you call a time-out? I tend not to because it will give the defense a chance to set up. Sometimes you call time-out and the official doesn't see it, and then you only have six seconds left, not ten. I will call a time-out if I see that "panic look." You only know that when you see it. I tell my players that when we are taking the last shot, I want an opportunity to win. Make sure you at least get a shot. I want to minimize the opportunities for a turnover, and I want to have two options to score.

DIAGRAM 4-2. THE TWELVE PLAY

DIAGRAM 4-3.

We call it "12" because we run it with 12 seconds on the clock. This doesn't give the other team time to get a rebound and go down and score. 3 is the shooter. 3 comes off the screen, and 2 pops the stack.

DIAGRAM 4-4.

We then have a triangle with 2, 3, and 4. 3 can shoot or pass inside to 4.

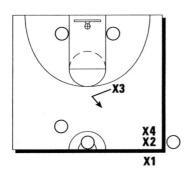

If that doesn't happen, 5 steps out and sets a screen for 1. If 1 has the shot, she takes it. If not, 5 rolls down the lane. This is simple, but I want it simple down the stretch. I don't want anything fancy.

DIAGRAM 4-5. MASTER CHARGE

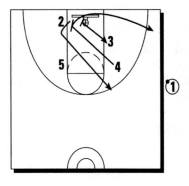

1 is the free-throw shooter who wants the ball when the game is on the line. Tell the official that you are going to do this. 3 runs hard in one direction, and 2 breaks toward the ball yelling for the ball. 1 sneaks up to the baseline and sets a screen hoping to take the charge. If the charge doesn't occur, 3 passes to 5 for the shot.

DIAGRAM 4-6. VISA

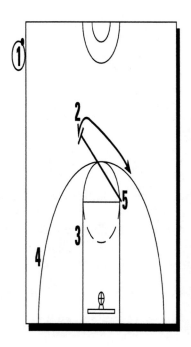

This is used with one or two seconds left in the game, and we must go the length of the floor. 3 must be able to run the baseline. Put shooters in the 4 and 5 positions. 3 must be able to throw the long pass.(Remember, this is desperation time.) If the game is tied, make sure that 3 throws the ball in the court. If there is no one on the ball, we use this. 1 breaks to the ball. 4 sets a pick for 2. 5 also sets a pick for 2. If no charge is called, 3 can pass to 2 for a shot. 3 can also pass to 4 or 5 breaking up in the middle.

DIAGRAM 4-7. FOOTBALL

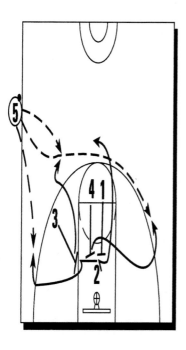

2, 3, and 4 break toward the ball but then set a triple screen near mid-court. 1 breaks to the basket off the triple screen. 2,3, and 4 must be defensed. They cannot be allowed to catch the ball at mid-court. 5 passes to 1. A nice thing about this pass is that it doesn't have to be accurate.

DIAGRAM 4-8.

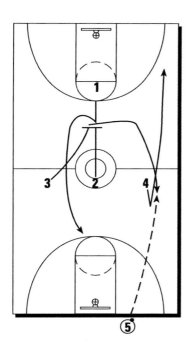

This can be used if you have five or six seconds. 2 sets a fake screen and breaks to mid-court. 5 also breaks to mid-court. Throw the ball to 5 and call time-out if no one else is open.

DIAGRAM 4-9.

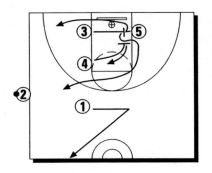

DIAGRAM 4-10.

At half-court. 3 is the shooter. 4 is the best post with back to basket. 5 is a decoy. 3 screens for 5. 4 screens for 3, so we pick the picker. 3 comes to the ball for the pass and the shot. 4 must turn and roll if 3 isn't open.

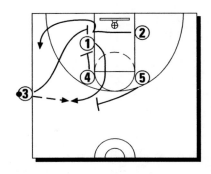

DIAGRAM 4-11.

This can be used against either a zone or a man. 2 is the shooter. 4 screens for 1, who breaks to the ball. 3 passes to 1 and sets a screen for 2. 1 can pass to 2 or use the screen by 5. This play seals off the entire back side, and 5 will roll to the basket.

This is for the three-point shot. 5 screens for 3. 3 breaks into the middle and then wraps around 4's screen. 2 passes to 3, or 2 can pass to 5 and then to 3.

DIAGRAM 4-12. THE BALL IS AT MID-

COURT

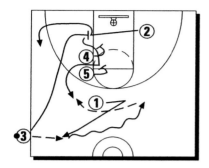

3 inbounds to 1, and 3 sets a low screen for 2. 4 and 5 then set staggered-picks for 3, who breaks to the three-point area as 1 attacks the basket. 1 can pass to 3, or 1 can also pass to 2. Another option is that 1 has the entire right side of the floor to drive.

DIAGRAM 4-13. ONE SECOND REMAINING

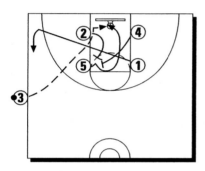

1 breaks to the corner. 2 and 4 set a double-screen for 5, who breaks for the basket for the lob from 3.

CHAPTER 5

SPECIAL SITUATIONS

DICK HARTER

I'm going to talk on a lot of different things. I want to start by giving you one of the toughest things in basketball, that is, *getting a shot for a key player* at a key time in the game. I'll give them to you by position. *You must plan the next play ahead.* When people take something away from you defensively, you must be ready to go to a play that takes advantage of their overcommitment. Then we will cover some out of bounds plays, some defensive ideas, and some defensive control patterns. For example, you can really do some things offensively if you move every defensive player to a different spot on the floor before you attack. How do we get someone the ball for a quick shot with only 10 or 15 seconds to go? Maybe some of the best things you do offensively, you should do with just one or two passes. Think about this. How many turnovers will you have if you make one or two passes and then the shot goes up?

DIAGRAM 5-1.

Point guard first. 2 is the best screener, 1 is the point guard. If 3 and 4 exchange, their defensive men will be concerned enough so that they will not sag too much. 5 steps up and sets a side-screen. 1 uses the screen and turns the corner for a layup. If the defensive player guarding 2 sees that, he will come over to stop 1. 1 then passes to 2 for the shot. Or 5's man may check 1, which means that 5 rolls to the basket on the *screen and roll play.* The key point in using screens is that you *must come off the screen tight.* You can't give the defense room to slide through.

DIAGRAM 5-2.

Rather than just exchanging on the weakside, *screen a rebounder.* 3 screens 4's man, so 4 is then free for an offensive rebound.

DIAGRAM 5-3.

Detroit uses this. 4 screens for 1. 5 and 3 set a double, 2 clears around the double, and 1 and 4 run a two-man play.

DIAGRAM 5-4.

This is what it looks like in the other direction.

DIAGRAM 5-5.

Another play for a point guard. 5 is your best screener. 1 dribbles toward the side. 1 must get down below the foul line. 1 reverses back using 5's screen. 5 rolls.

DIAGRAM 5-6.

Many players wait too long to make the pass to the open player. Assume that 2's man comes over to stop the dribble. The defense will give you the pass to 2. Too many players wait until this defensive man is right in their face. Don't wait. Make the pass when he is still two steps away.

DIAGRAM 5-7.

Now a play for the off-guard. When you use such a formation, always put the same people in the same place. Keep it simple. 3 screens across for 2. 5 then sets a second screen and 2 comes off the *staggered double-screen*. Players can handle one screen, but not two.

DIAGRAM 5-8. OFF GUARD PLAY

This is good for an athletic guard. 2 gets three screens. 3 back-screens and there is a possible lob. 4 comes across and sets another screen and then 5 sets a third screen. 1 passes to 2 for the shot.

DIAGRAM 5-9.

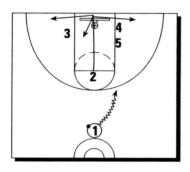

Put your good off-guard at the foul line. Send 2 to the baseline and he has a choice of the double-screen, the single screen or else coming back to the ball.

DIAGRAM 5-10.

For the small forward, #3. 3 crosses and screens for 2. But that is a *diversion*. Then 4 and 5 set a *double down-screen* for 3. Things that look like they are going to do one thing and then do another are good. 1 looks to 2. 2 may be open.

DIAGRAM 5-11.

This is tougher timing. 5 and 4 are shoulder to shoulder. 3 must wait for 4 and 5 to come to him. If the defense switches, 4 or 5 come to the ball.

DIAGRAM 5-12.

This is a good rule for people receiving the screens. *You are better going late than you are going early.* Look what happens if you go early. If you go two steps too soon, you will get the ball at 17 feet.

DIAGRAM 5-13.

If you go too late, you will get the ball much closer to the basket. When I do camps, I give a talk telling the kids to get their shot *one step closer*. It's our job as coaches to try to get our players the best available shot. The longer you wait, the better off you are.

DIAGRAM 5-14.

Another play for the *small forward*. You start on one side of the floor and come back the other way. 1 dribbles to the side. 2 runs a shuffle cut off of 4's screen. 5 and 3 set a stack down low.

DIAGRAM 5-15.

3 uses 5 and pops out as 1 reverses to the other side of the floor off of a pick by 4. The timing must be there, 3 must not pop out too early. When we went side to side, we were 15% more effective in the NBA.

DIAGRAM 5-16.

Another way to get the ball to the small forward is the curl action. 3 starts low. 1 dribbles down and passes to 3 while 4 and 2 exchange.

DIAGRAM 5-17.

If the defender goes over the top, 5 steps up and 3 flattens out to the corner.

DIAGRAM 5-18.

If the defense trails, we call it tagging. 3 curls around 5.

DIAGRAM 5-19.

If the defense cheats and goes behind 5 before 3 does, 3 pops back for the layup.

DIAGRAM 5-20.

I call this the "Dog Play." This is for the big forward. 1 passes to 3 and 2 runs a shuffle cut off of 5. Don't ever run your man off of a screen on a shuffle cut. *You must walk him into the screen.* You want to teach your players to read the defense. That's the first option.

DIAGRAM 5-21.

1 makes an inside cut. 3 passes to 1 or to 5.

DIAGRAM 5-22.

5 takes a dribble. 4 comes to the elbow and then screens down for 1. 1 pops out and gets the pass from 5. 1 can then pass inside to 4. 4 has his man sealed on his back.

DIAGRAM 5-23.

If 1 does not pass to 4, 5 and 3 set a double-screen for 2 who gets pass from 1.

DIAGRAM 5-24.

Here is your *counter*. 2 can also take one step up, and then reverse using 4's screen and get a pass from 1.

DIAGRAM 5-25. DIAGONAL

Here is one for post up. 4 screens for 3. 5 comes off 4's back. 2 must get away, so 2 comes across and sets screen for 3. 1 passes to 5 or to 3.

DIAGRAM 5-26.

5 is on the post, 3 behind the double-screen. 1 still has the ball. 3 starts up, goes low and you have a counter play off of "Diagonal."

DIAGRAM 5-27.

1 goes left on the dribble. 3 sets the angle *up-screen* as 2 and 4 switch.

DIAGRAM 5-28.

Let's talk a little defense. This is the way we defend a *low cross.* This may be the toughest thing to defend. 2 screens for 1. We want X1 to go low to the block. Always go low. X2 steps up and gives help and bumps 1. This keeps X2 high.

CHAPTER 6

QUICK HITTERS— SET PLAYS

BILL HERRION

"1-4"

DIAGRAM 6-1.

Enter out of a *1-4 set*. 1's dribble will push 2 through to the basket. 1 can look to turn the corner on the wing with the dribble.

DIAGRAM 6-2.

5 will step out from the elbow and screen on the ball for 1 on the wing. 1 uses 5's screen. As 1 puts the ball on the floor to use the screen, 3 and 4 will *stagger-screen* for 2 on the opposite side.

1 will look to turn the corner and create off 5's screen. 1 will look to 2 off the *stagger-screen* by 3 and 4. 5 will screen on the ball and roll or flare for a shot.

DIAGRAM 6-3. NEW ALIGNMENT

QUICK HITTERS - SET PLAYS

DIAGRAM 6-4.

1 will *dribble-push* at 2. Look for a possible backdoor to 2 if overplayed on the wing. 2 will cut through to the opposite mid-baseline area.

As 1 dribble-pushes to the wing, 3 will shuffle-cut off 4's high screen looking for a possible layup or post-up on the block.

Once 3 clears 4, 4 will open and step out to the top of the key for ball reversal.

DIAGRAM 6-5.

On the pass from 1 to 4 on a step-out, 5 will screen down for 2. 2 will walk the defender along the baseline and read the defense coming off 5's down-screen. Look for straight pop, curl or fade.

If 2 does not have a shot off the downscreen, look for 5.

"2"–Options if 4 is denied for ball reversal.

DIAGRAM 6-6.

4 screens on the ball for 1. 1 will dribble-push 2 through and get the ball to the wing, foul line extended.

3 will shuffle-cut off 4 to the ballside block.

DIAGRAM 6-7.

As 4 steps out for ball reversal, if 4 is *denied*, 4 will go screen on the ball for 1. 1 has to keep the dribble alive on the wing. 1 will come off 4's screen. As 1 comes off the screen on the ball, 5 will screen down for 2.

4-STAGGER-SCREEN WITH 4 FOR 2.

DIAGRAM 6-8.

Same as above, 1 will dribble-push the ball to the wing. As 4 steps out for ball reversal, if denied, he will back-cut and stagger-screen for 2 with 5.

"3" PUSH

DIAGRAM 6-9.

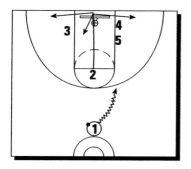

1 will dribble-push at 2. Look for a possible backdoor to 2 if overplayed. 2 will screen for 5 on the front of rim. 5 will look to come to the baseline side off 2's screen.

1 will look to 5 inside for back to basket. As 2 screens for 5, 4 will screen the screener for 2.

DIAGRAM 6-10.

2 will come off 4's screen looking for a *jump shot*. This play is designed to get the ball to 2 and 5, who are our best offensive players.

DIAGRAM 6-11.

If 2 has no shot, look for 4 or reverse to 3 and go into the *motion offense*.

"3" HITCH

DIAGRAM 6-12.

Enter out of the exact same set as *3 push*.

DIAGRAM 6-13.

If the defense on 2 starts cheating on 4's screen the screener, look to bring 2 off 5's baseline screen.

DIAGRAM 6-14.

Enter out of same set as *3 push*. If you have a 2 or 3 man who can post-up or who has a mismatch, this is a good option. 1 will dribble-push at 2. 2 will backdoor and start to screen for 5, then curl back and look to post on the block.

DIAGRAM 6-15.

4 will down-screen for 5, looking to bring 5 to the top of the key for a shot on the high/low.

DIAGRAM 6-16.

Enter out of the *box set*. We are really looking to get the ball to 2 or 5. 1 will dribble-push to the wing. 1 can use 4's high screen if defensive pressure is hard. 1 has to get the ball to the foul line extended for a good passing angle into post.

As 1 dribble-pushes to the wing, 2 will diagonally up-screen for 5. 5 will look to come off the screen hard to the block for a post-up. The first look is inside to 5.

DIAGRAM 6-17.

4 will screen the screener for 2, looking for 2 at the top of the key for a jump shot.

DIAGRAM 6-18.

3 will step outside on a weakside part of the floor to take the defensive help away. If 2 has no shot, look for 4 on a duck-in into motion offense.

"BOX STAGGER"

DIAGRAM 6-19.

Enter out of the same set as *"Box."* Put a shooter at the 3 spot. 1 will enter the ball with a dribble to the wing. As 1 dribble-enters, 2 will diagonally up-screen for 5. Still look for 5 on the block.

DIAGRAM 6-20.

Instead of stepping 3 out wide, keep him on the block. 2 and 4 will stagger for 3, looking to bring 3 off the stagger for a shot. 2 will space out after screening and go into motion offense.

"HAWK" VS. MAN

DIAGRAM 6-21.

This is a quick hitter for our 3 man vs. man-to-man.

We enter out of a *stack set*. 3 will look to rub defense off of 4 and pop to the wing. We want 3 to touch the ball on the wing to make X3 play him.

DIAGRAM 6-22.

1 will make an entry pass and replace himself. On the pass from 3 to 1, 4 will step out and back-screen 3. 1 will drive the ball once or twice toward the middle. 3 will come off the back-screen and look to get into the lane. After 4 back-screens, he will look to re-screen for 3. 3 has the option to come off the single or the double. Most of the time, 3 should look to come off the single screen.

DIAGRAM 6-23.

3 has to *read* the defense and use the screen the proper way. 3 can pop out, bump or curl.

DIAGRAM 6-24.

If X4 looks to *cheat* out on 3 off of the screen. we must look to go directly from 1 to 4 on block down the seam.

"DOUBLE" —MAN ENTRY

DIAGRAM 6-25.

1 comes off a screen by 4 as 2 screens away for 5. As 1 comes off of 4's screen, 4 and 3 set a double-screen for 2.

"DOUBLE SPECIAL" —MAN ENTRY

DIAGRAM 6-26.

2 and 5 change spots. 1 comes off screen set by 4, and 5 screens away for 2.

DIAGRAM 6-27.

As 1 comes off 4's screen, 3 then back-screens for 4. 1 skip-passes to 4, who has flared for the three-point shot.

"RICHMOND"

DIAGRAM 6-28.

This play is designed to get the ball to 5 on the block or 2 off of a *staggered screen.* 1 will bring the ball off 4's screen with a dribble. 1 has the option to turn the corner to the basket. If not, get the ball to the foul line extended so he has an angle to feed the post. As 1 brings the ball off the high screen, 2 will screen away in front of the rim for 5. 5 will read the defense, but mostly come off 2's screen baseline side.

DIAGRAM 6-29.

1's first look is to 5 on the block in-side. As 2 screens away for 5, 3 and 4 will stagger-screen for 2. 2 will screen for 5, then look to come off the stagger-screen for a shot.

DIAGRAM 6-30.

3 will space out and balance the floor, and 4 will *duck-in* hard and go into motion offense.

CHAPTER 7

SIDE OUT-OF-BOUNDS FRONT COURT

BILL HERRION

"RICHMOND"

DIAGRAM 7-1.

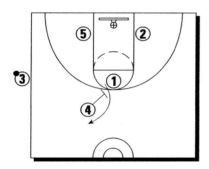

We start with 4 screening in for 1.

DIAGRAM 7-2.

On the pass from 3 to 1, 1 will come off 4's high screen, looking to get the ball to the foul line extended to feed the post.

DIAGRAM 7-3.

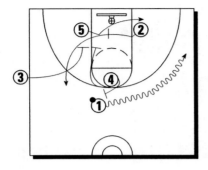

As 1 brings the ball off 4's high screen, 2 will screen away for 5 in front of rim. The first look is from 1 to 5 inside. 5 should come off 4's screen baseline side. As 2 screens for 5 inside, 3 and 4 will stagger-screen for 2. 2 will look to come off the stagger-screen for the shot.

DIAGRAM 7-4.

3 and 4 will *split and balance* the floor into motion offense.

"BELOW"

DIAGRAM 7-5.

We usually run this play if we need a three-point shot at the end of game. 1 will take the ball out-of-bounds. As the official hands the ball to 1, 2 and 4 will set a stagger-screen for 3. 3 will come off a stagger-screen looking for the shot. If we need a three-point shot, 3 will get to the three-point line.

DIAGRAM 7-6.

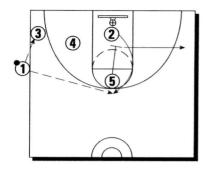

5 will screen down and screen the screener for 2. Once 3 comes off 2's screen, 2 will come off 5 looking for a shot at the top of the key.

DIAGRAM 7-7.

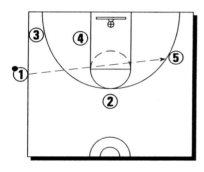

Put a good perimeter shooter in 5's spot, 5 will screen down, then fade to the opposite three point line. Three options exist:

- 3 off stagger-screen by 2 and 4.
- 2 off 5's screen the screener.
- 5 down-screen and fade skip-pass.

DIAGRAM 7-8.

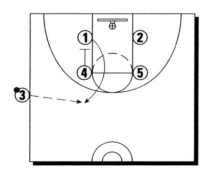

Enter out of a *Box Set*. 3 will take the ball out. As the official hands the ball to 3, 4 screens down for 1 on the ballside.

DIAGRAM 7-9.

On the pass from 3 to 1, 1 will center the ball with a dribble to the middle of the floor. 1 centers the ball, 2 will take his defender into the middle of the lane.

DIAGRAM 7-10.

2 has the option of coming off 5's down-screen or off of 4 and 3's stagger-screen. 2 has to read the defense and take what the defense gives him.

"ABOVE"

DIAGRAM 7-11.

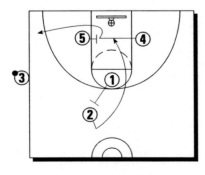

We run this when the ball is above the top of the key. As the official hands the ball to 3, the offense will move. The first look is directly to 5 if the defense plays behind. 4 will come off 5's screen on the block to the ball-side corner. If 4 is a good perimeter shooter, 4 can look for the shot. 1 will back-screen for 2. 2 will take a step away, then come off of a back-screen, looking for the throw over the top for a layup.

DIAGRAM 7-12.

3 looks for his *alternate* options: 5-4-2. The key feed is if X1 stays tight on the back-screen, 2 will be open over the top.

DIAGRAM 7-13.

If the *lob* is not open, 3 will inbound to 1 on a step out. 3 will follow the pass and screen on the ball for 1. 2 will come off a stagger-screen by 4 and 5 for a shot.

"2"

DIAGRAM 7-14.

2 inbounds the ball. 3 and 5 stack on the strongside block. 1 is on the opposite side in the foul line area.

DIAGRAM 7-15.

5 pops to the corner, and 1 back-screens for 4. If 2 can hit 4 for a layup, he does. If not, he hits 5 in the corner.

DIAGRAM 7-16.

2 steps into the lane, and 5 reverses the ball out immediately to 1. 2 comes off a screen by 5 and 3 or the single screen by 4 opposite.

RUN AND JUMP PRESS

JIM JOHNSON

I had a team coming back that didn't have great shooters, so we decided that we wanted organized chaos. We were going to press organized chaos and hopefully teams weren't going to practice organized chaos, so we were going to have the advantage. I've always called it a man-to-man full-court trap. Other people called it a run and jump. We used this to create offense. The players really liked it. Everyone got to play. I would substitute another five players about every three minutes.

If you use this, you must commit to it and spend a lot of time on it. We spent at least one hour each practice on this. You must have kids who are willing to work. There are rules. Here they are: Say, push, deny, trap, rotate, turn and run. It's man-to-man. I did not know where our players were going to be. They went wherever their player went. The only thing is you must have a good defensive point guard. You must have that. You must be able to control the dribbler.

DIAGRAM 8-1.

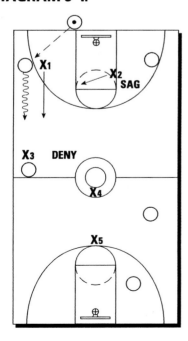

We do not deny the inbounds pass. But we do not allow the pass into the lane. X1 is an arm's length away and will use the sideline. We want the ball dribbled up the sideline. If the dribbler picks up the dribble, X 1 is after the ball. While the ball is being dribbled, X2 sags to the line of the ball, this is the rule for the person closest to the ball on the weakside. The strongside player X3., denies all passes. When the dribbler has her back turned, X2 is coming to trap. X1 is enticing her up the sideline. If the dribbler can't make the pass up the sideline, what are the possibilities? X1 needs to keep the dribbler on the sideline. She cannot let her use the cross-over dribble and get into the middle.

Anything behind the back, between the legs, reverse pivot, that is the problem of the person coming to trap.

DIAGRAM 8-2.

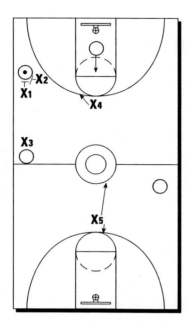

If the dribbler stops, X1 jumps in front and X2 sets the trap at a ninety degree angle. Don't foul because that gets them out of the trap. Don't slap the ball out-of-bounds because they are then out of the trap. When they are in the trap, and they have picked up their dribble, let them go. We don't know for sure where anyone is going to be because we are in a man press. But if you are the next closest player X4, you must rotate part way up. X5 also adjusts. X4 and X5 are covering three players. X1 and X2 must be tight so she cannot make the long diagonal pass. X4 and X5 cannot over-rotate. It is basic weakside defense, see the players and the ball. If we don't get the pass, turn and run. That is your rule. Don't turn and look, turn and run.

DIAGRAM 8-3.

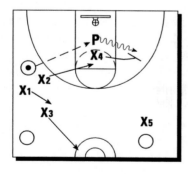

On the *reversal*, the ball goes over X2's head so she turns and runs. X4 has the dribbler and is the same as Diagram 8-2 except it is on the other side. X5 denies the pass down the sideline, X4 controls the dribbler, X2 is coming to trap, X3 sprints to the safety position and X1 is sagging to the middle.

DIAGRAM 8-4.

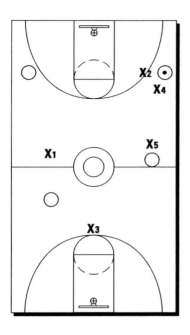

When the trap is made, this is how it looks.

DIAGRAM 8-5.

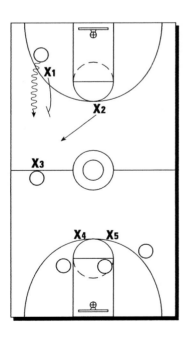

If the offensive team clears out and tries to bring the ball up with just one person, the same rules apply. X2 is the last person out, so she does not leave. X3 will overplay the strong sideline, X1 is controlling the dribbler down the sideline, X2 is coming over to trap. X4 and X5 are covering the other three players who have gone deep.

DIAGRAM 8-6.

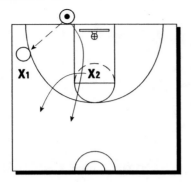

When the offense inbounded and then the inbounder went deep when we were trying to deny the return pass, they would kill us.

DIAGRAM 8-7.

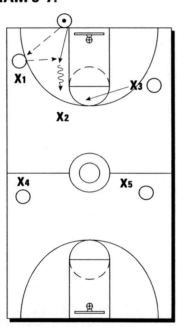

When that happens, we let the inbounder get the return pass and then we trap her. X3 sags to the ball, and we are in the same positions. X1 will hustle back and may be able to steal from behind.

DIAGRAM 8-8.

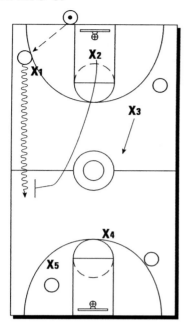

Sometimes the dribbler would *blast* up the sideline. We let her go. She must stop sometime, and then we will trap. X1 and X2 must run at the proper angle. X2 cannot get behind and chase. X2 must take the proper angle.

DIAGRAM 8-9.

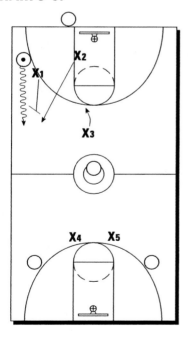

The hardest thing to cover is the *flash* into the middle of the floor. X5's player will never get the ball. If she does, there is something seriously wrong. So we forget her almost completely. X2 comes over to trap; X1 is applying pressure. X3 must come up, and X5 must come all the way up to cover the middle person.

DIAGRAM 8-10.

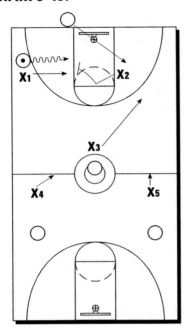

If the person dribbles to the middle, X2 will be sagging into the middle and now X1 and X2 will trap. X3 rotates up; X4 rotates and covers the middle. X5 moves up. All the players must be moving. If the dribbler is coming slow, it is X1's job to make her go fast. We can also do this on a half-court basis.

DIAGRAM 8-11. DRILLS.

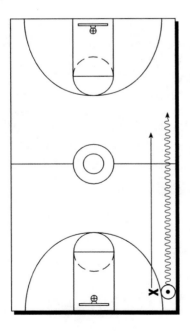

We had everyone do this drill, not just the point guards, because if the ball were reversed, then someone other than the point guard would be in this position. The dribbler would go for the layup, and it was strictly one-on-one. We put rules on it. The dribbler could only go straight down the court with the right hand. Then we would allow the cross-over dribble also, but nothing else. Then we would add the hesitation dribble.

Question: What happens if someone sets a screen for the dribbler going down the sideline?

Answer: We will switch.

DIAGRAM 8-12. 1 ON 2

We told X1 and X2, trap the dribbler. The dribbler could use the entire court. We wanted to trap her into a corner. It was important that the trap be made at 90 degrees because the dribbler could escape.

DIAGRAM 8-13. 2-ON-3

Then we added a second person on offense vs. X3 on defense. We would trap and then try to steal the pass.

DIAGRAM 8-14.

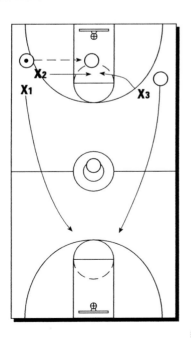

We also play *3-on-3 full court*. The only rule is the offense can't cut strongside. We inbound the ball and try to trap. When the pass is made, X3 goes for the steal. If the pass was completed, X2 and X3 would try to trap. When the ball went out of the trap, X1 should turn and sprint deep to cover.

DIAGRAM 8-15. 4-ON-4

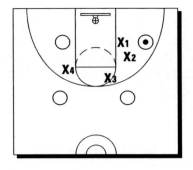

There will be two players on the trap, and two players trying to steal. The offensive players could not move. Anytime the ball was passed, all defensive players had to move. Later on, we would allow the offensive players to move.

CHAPTER 9

OUT-OF-BOUNDS UNDERNEATH

LON KRUGER

Y ou cannot just take what we do and copy it. You must gear it to your personnel's ability, what they do and don't do well. It allows us to move people around, to run the same action for any number of different players. Our point guard is 1; 2 and 3 are swing men; 4 is the power forward and 5 is the post. We have several *"options"* for out-of-bounds underneath. We always inbound the ball with the point guard. These are all against a man-to-man defense.

DIAGRAM 9-1. STRONG ACTION

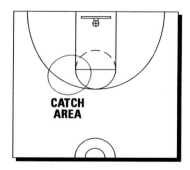

We inbound the ball to the "catch area." We may have to pass to the wing first, but we want the ball to go to this area.

DIAGRAM 9-2.

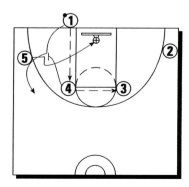

We inbound to the *catch area.* We are then going to make a guard-to-guard pass. On the pass from 4 to 3, 5 shuffle-cuts off the screen of 1. 4 then down-screens for 1 and then posts.

DIAGRAM 9-3.

3 then passes to 1. 1 looks to 4 or 5. You have *three looks;* the *shuffle-cutter,* the *point guard,* and the *pass inside.* We can put any player in any of those spots.

DIAGRAM 9-4.

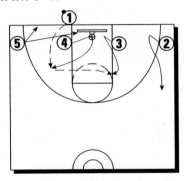

If we want to *shuffle-cut* the post man, we call *"43 strong."* That means 4 receives the pass. The big man, not in the call (5), will be in the corner on the ballside. The perimeter man not in the call will be corner opposite (2). 4 and 3 will influence to the baseline. 4 moves to the elbow to receive the pass. 3 breaks to the other elbow to get the pass from 4. When 4 passes to 3, 5 shuffle-cuts off of 1's pick.

DIAGRAM 9-5.

4 down-screens for 1 for the jumper.

DIAGRAM 9-6. "35 STRONG"

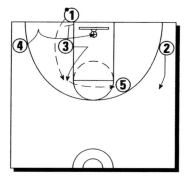

If 3 is a good post-up man, run this. 3 gets the pass in the *catch area*, and makes the guard-to-guard pass to 5. 3 then *down-screens* for 1 after 4 makes his shuffle-cut. 3 posts-up.

DIAGRAM 9-7.

How can this be stopped? If you start with four men on the baseline, the other team must get on the top of four. But, you have the basket there to keep people honest. If that occurs, we call *"50"* which is the *automatic lob.* 4 takes one step back into the defense and knifes to the goal. 4 can also start up the lane and turn and loop back to the basket.

DIAGRAM 9-8.

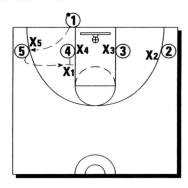

Put 1's defensive man on top. This is an automatic. This keys 4 to seal X1, and 1 passes to 5 who makes the return pass to 1 for the shot.

DIAGRAM 9-9.

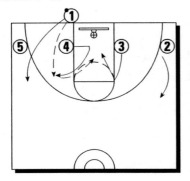

Some teams try to take away the guard-to-guard pass. 3 comes high and then goes backdoor to receive the pass from 4. 2 must move to keep the defensive player away from the ball.

DIAGRAM 9-10. "43 COUNTER"

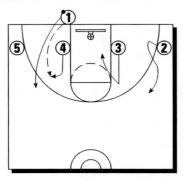

We use this against a team that overplays. On the *"counter"* call, 2 steps *hard and high*. 3 must *backcut*. The ball goes from 1-4-3, or from 1-4-2-3. 2 feeds 3 as 3 posts.

DIAGRAM 9-11. "24 WEAK"

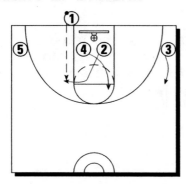

We use this for a good perimeter shooter. We start with 2 and 4 stacked in the lane. 2 can use 4 to get into the catch area. 4 then goes to the opposite elbow.

DIAGRAM 9-12.

Now instead of shuffle-cutting, 5 sets a flare-pick for 2. 2 flares for the skip-pass from 4. 1 goes higher than the free-throw line extended. He must take his defensive man away from the basket. 2 and 5 have the entire side of the floor. 5 rolls to the post area. 5 can also pick for 4, who can come to the top of the key.

DIAGRAM 9-13.

5's defensive man usually steps out to help on 2. We then *"slip the flare-pick,"* and 5 cuts to the basket for the pass from 4.

DIAGRAM 9-14. "42 WEAK SLIP"

5 picks for 4. The others must keep their people out of the way. They must play act and influence their men out of the area. We can run this play for any of our players. We can call *35 weak, 52 weak, 24 weak.* You can run that jumper for anyone. When your opponents walk through some of your plays, you can give it a completely different look by changing the positions of your men.

DIAGRAM 9-15. "WEAK 42 OPPOSITE"

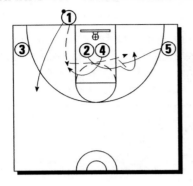

"Weak 42 opposite" is a variation. This is a jump shot for 2. 4 uses 2 and goes to the catch area. On the "opposite" call, the big man not in the call goes to the corner opposite. 5 flare-screens for 2. 1 goes to the ballside of the floor keeping his man away from the action. The ball goes from 1-4-2.

DIAGRAM 9-16. "42 OPPOSITE SLIP"

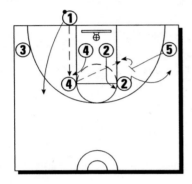

5 can slip that for a pass from 4.

DIAGRAM 9-17. "24 POST"

With a strong point guard, post him. Whoever you want feeding the post, have him catch the ball. It looks like "strong action." 1 passes to 2 who fakes the pass to 4. 5 makes the shuffle-cut; 2 passes to 1 who has posted up. 5 cuts to get a part of the defensive man of 1.

DIAGRAM 9-18.

The entire side of the floor is open for 2 after the pass to 1. Anytime you feed the pass, you must move. Occupy the defense.

DIAGRAM 9-19. "42 POST"

We set it up so that 2 always feeds the post. 5 will always be on the side of 2. The ball goes from 1-4-2.

DIAGRAM 9-20.

Sometimes 2 must dribble to improve the angle to feed the post as shown on this *"24 post."*

DIAGRAM 9-21. "25 GUT"

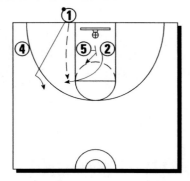

5 sets pick for 2 who gets the ball in the *catch area.* 2 then looks low for 5 who steps to the ball. The big man not in the call goes to the *corner ballside.* 1 sprints out to get his defensive man out of the way. Everything is spread along the baseline and 5 is isolated.

DIAGRAM 9-22. "50"

This is a *lob* in front of the goal. 5 can V-cut back to the goal or make a loop. We want 5 going toward the goal when he catches the ball. Whoever is on the opposite block, must dive hard to the baseline to clear the area.

DIAGRAM 9-23. "50 SEAL"

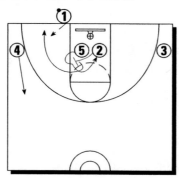

5 steps into the open area. 2 sets a back-pick for the same type of action as a *"50."* Sometimes 2 is open for the shot.

DIAGRAM 9-24.

If 2 gets the pass but doesn't have a shot, 5 steps back to the ball.

DIAGRAM 9-25. "53 STRONG"

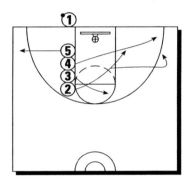

We can line up this way also. 2 breaks opposite; 4 goes to the corner; 3 goes to opposite elbow and 5 to the catch area.

DIAGRAM 9-26.

After the shuffle-cut, for a variation, 1 can back-pick for 4 who breaks down and posts-up. The ball can go from 2-4-2-1 or 2-4-2-1-4.

DIAGRAM 9-27.

Against a zone we can run *"24 weak."* It is a little different. Usually against a zone we must inbound the ball through 5, who then passes to 2 in the *catch area.* 2 passes to 4, and 5 screens the top man in the zone. 2 steps wide.

DIAGRAM 9-28.

The baseline man in the zone now has both 1 and 2 to guard. 4 passes to 2 who can pass to 1.

DIAGRAM 9-29.

We can run *"42 opposite"* against a zone. 5 is in opposite corner. 1 inbounds to 4. 5 seals the top man in the zone. 1 goes to opposite corner as 2 comes off the pick of 5. 4 passes to 2 who can pass to 1.

DIAGRAM 9-30.

"*42 strong*" against a zone means that we lob. The ball goes from 1-4-2. 5 shuffle-cuts high to influence the middle man of the zone. 1 seals the back man in the zone, and 4 goes to the basket for the lob. After the pick by 1, 1 steps out wide.

DIAGRAM 9-31.

Sometimes on the "*24 weak*" against a zone after the pass from 1 to 2 to 4, 5 sets the screen on the top man of the zone and then breaks into the middle of the lane for the jumper.

DIAGRAM 9-32.

We can run a "*42 strong*" from the sideline out-of-bounds. We inbound the ball with the man who is not in the call. 1 gets the pass coming off of the double pick. 1 dribbles to the wing.

DIAGRAM 9-33.

4 receives the pass from 1 in the *catch area*. 2 goes opposite. 1 goes to the post; 5 shuffle-cuts out of the corner, and 3 is wide opposite. So, we run exactly the same thing from the side. You can run any of those actions from the sideline inbounds.

CHAPTER 10

INBOUND PLAYS

ANDY LANDERS

What do your inbound plays look like when you line up? Are you scouted? Can they tell what you are running just by the way that you set up? We want everything to look the same.

DIAGRAM 10-1.

2 is the shooter. 4 runs at this player and 3 replaces 4.

DIAGRAM 10-2.

3 breaks all the way to the baseline. 2 to 3 to 1, who broke straight out. 4 continued across the lane and sets a double-screen with 5 for 2. 3 will skip-pass to 2.

DIAGRAM 10-3.

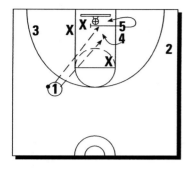

After you run this, the defense will try to slip a man over or under the screen. If this happens, 1 does not pass to 2. 5 will screen in, and 4 will get the pass from 1.

DIAGRAM 10-4.

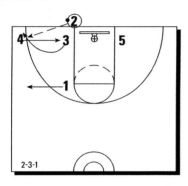

Starts out the same way; 4 runs in, 3 bananas to the baseline, but 4 stays at the block. 1 breaks out, and the ball goes from 2 to 3 to 1.

DIAGRAM 10-5.

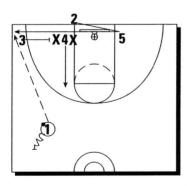

4 screens the inside man, 3 screens the outside player and 1 passes to 2. But before the pass to 2, 1 wags back as if she is going somewhere. 2 must first fake the same move as in the previous play. 4 steps up the lane. This is important because that holds the middle man in the zone.

DIAGRAM 10-6.

Here is another set. 4 and 5 cut first and can screen. 2 will be the best option.

DIAGRAM 10-7. "ORANGE"

Against a man defense. Most people will guard in the lane.

DIAGRAM 10-8.

What do you do if 2 breaks off of 3? If you don't switch, you trail. 1 passes to 2, who either goes to the corner or curls.

DIAGRAM 10-9.

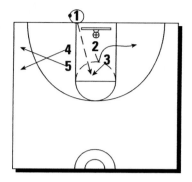

If you switch, 2 goes to the corner and 1 passes to 3. 4 and 5 get out of the way.

DIAGRAM 10-10. "BLUE"

2 screens for 3. The ball goes from 1 to 3.

DIAGRAM 10-11. SIDE-OUT

2 is the best one-on-one player. 5 screens down and 2 comes up. 3 passes to 2.

DIAGRAM 10-12.

1 screens the inbounder, who breaks to the corner. 4 screens across for 5. As soon as 2 got the ball she started to drive. She has the entire side to go one-on-one. If we get cut off on the drive, 5 will come off of 4's screen. 2 can pass to 5 or to 3 for the three-point shot.

DIAGRAM 10-13.

For the three-point shot, 2 is the shooter. 2 breaks high off of 4. 1 dribbles to the wing and then dribbles back. 2 sets a screen for 1. 4 back-screens for 3, who goes to the wing. Screen the screener and pass against the grain.

CHAPTER 11

SPECIAL SITUATIONS, TIME AND SCORE

BILLIE MOORE

How much time do you spend on all the situations that come up in a game? If you are going to have a play for the last 5 seconds, the last 10 seconds, for coming out of the locker room at halftime, etc., my approach to this (what I evolved into in my last few years of coaching), is trying to take something like a set that you might run in your half-court offense and run it for all situations. I have a zone attack that I run against all zones. I don't believe in having a zone attack that you run against an odd front and a different attack for an even front. Hopefully, you have an attack that will allow you to play against a match-up, an odd front, or an even front. It's the same thing I talked about earlier. The more you ask them to learn, the more watered down they become. If you can take one or two things and teach it, you are better off. Today, how to attack the match-up is the problem. When you get to what you are going to do against a zone, you must also include what you are going to do out-of-bounds, on the end line or the sideline. Do I have things that are just out-of-bounds against a zone, or do I have things that work against both the zone and a man defense?

Same thing when you talk about your man package. Maybe your transition is your primary attack. What are you going to do when you must set up in a half-court set? The most difficult pass to make in this set is the entry pass. I must have something that gives me more than one option. We got to the point where our number one offense was our transition game. We looked to run off a make, a miss, a turnover, anything.

We found that our secondary break became our *primary offense.* It just meant that it started from the endline instead of coming down and setting up in a half-court offense. I liked it because we were coming down the floor and going right into the attack. When you get into time/score, you must decide what you are going to do in a comeback situation. When do I start it? How many points down and how much time is left? I must know my personnel, and their ability.

On the other hand, there is a time/score situation when I am milking the clock. I must decide on the last-second play. Do I have something in my plan for a last-second shot? I'm telling you that you can call time-out and draw the neatest play, but they are not going to go out and do it. Two will remember it; two won't, and the other one doesn't have any idea what is going on. So, it's a lot easier if you can just say to them what they are going to run. How many of you find time to work on end of the game situations daily in practice? Not many hands are up. This becomes a time problem.

One of the things I started to do the last few years of coaching is play three-minute games. Put any score on the clock you want, and then give them a three-minute situation. That will allow you to work on these situations. If you suddenly get a game and you start yelling "green, green" because they need to foul and you haven't had to do it in your first 10 games, they won't have any idea what it means. But if you have practiced it during some three-minute games and set up that situation, they will do it.

How about free throws? What do you do with the other team on the line and five seconds on the clock? What do you do if it is made or missed? Do your players know? What if you are down by one? What do you want to do? Do your players know what you want to do? Do you call time-out? You must make that decision. But you should make it on the practice floor in a three-minute game. Your players have the ability to run what you want because you have worked on it.

DIAGRAM 11-1.

We come down in our transition, our secondary break. The point guard comes to the side. We have choices about what we can do with the pass to the wing, the pass to the lag (#4), or a dribble out to the wing. So, we have more than one choice.

DIAGRAM 11-2.

Let's say we run our curl option or our look option. 1 dribbles toward 2; 2 comes off the screens of 5 and 4 and runs the loop. We now have the possibility of a 1 and 5 two-man play. If 2 is a good shooter, 1 passes back for the shot.

DIAGRAM 11-3.

We never let 1 get below the forty-five degree angle unless she is taking it to the basket or is feeding the post. Don't let your wings set up in the corners; it is difficult to reverse the ball from the corners. When we run our shooting drills, we run some for the point guard attacking the glass.

DIAGRAM 11-4.

1 can reverse to 2; we run a side post. 4 screens; 2 dribbles off the screen. 3 can stay, and 2 and 3 run a two-man game, or 3 can go to the corner. We run this same set from out of bounds on the sideline, after a time-out.

DIAGRAM 11-5.

We take this skill with 4 and 2 and work on *reading the screen*. Do they switch? Probably not because you have big/small. There is a philosophy on screening. If you screen big/big or small/small, you will get switching. Make your screens small/big, or big/small. Then you force the defense to do something other than switch. If they trail, 2 will penetrate. If they shoot the gap, we automatically read that and set a quarter screen.

DIAGRAM 11-6.

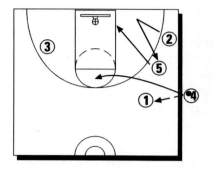

We run a variation of this from out-of-bounds. 4 inbounds to 1. We can run a curl. Or, 1 dribbles toward the middle. 2 pops out and 5 is on the post.

DIAGRAM 11-7.

4 comes over and we run the same thing.

DIAGRAM 11-8.

Out of the same philosophy, keep 5 low.

DIAGRAM 11-9.

Now we can reverse the ball. 1 passes to 4, reverse it and post up 5. 2 back-picks for 4 for the lob pass. If the lob isn't there, 4 comes back out. Now, we run the counter.

DIAGRAM 11-10.

1 to 4 to 3. 4 and 1 set a double-screen for 2. 5 comes to the ball. Transition.

I prefer not to call time-out in the last few seconds. We will run one of these options. And we have the same philosophy from out-of-bounds. We don't try to just get the ball in from out-of-bounds. We will run our offense from there. We try to score. In 25 years of coaching, making the entry pass hasn't gotten any easier, so you need more than one option. We run the same attack against a zone. The hardest thing in coaching is to get your players to play basketball and not play plays. The more plays you give them, the more you make them play plays. Give them the structure and let them play. Remember, run those three-minute games. Recognize the defense, man or zone, and run it. But you practice it. And you don't have too many things to practice because you haven't given them a play for every situation.

CHAPTER 12

SITUATION BASKETBALL

PAUL SANDERFORD

Normally, the people who come to clinics are the good coaches. All the bad coaches are somewhere else. I have been in your situation. I was in a junior college for six years, and I had no assistants. I was my staff.

How do you practice "*situations*?" When do you start practicing situations? What are we talking about? Time and score. I laminate 3 x 5 note cards with all types of situations. This one has thirty-four seconds, down three, our ball, out-of-bounds, backcourt, end line. I have about 40 of these. When I come to practice, I don't bring all of the cards. If I want to work on out-of-bounds sideline, those are the cards I bring. We play a little game; kids still like to play games at the college level. We play "pick a card," but I'm going to dictate what card they are going to pick.

I know what I want to work on. How do you do this? Do your kids know *what defense* you're going to play if you are two down? Do they know how you are going to play situations? If you are going to wait until there is a time-out before you put something in, you are not going to be very successful. I like to start the game by gaining the advantage.

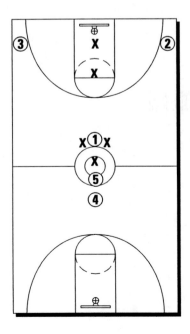

DIAGRAM 12-1.

This is a play I use to start the game. 5 is my jumper. I put 2 and 3 in the corners. This is if I think that I can get the tap. I want the coaching advantage to start with. If you are my opponent, you must make an adjustment right now. *How would you set your defense*? What would you do? Let's put them this way. The coach is making adjustments and by the time the ball goes up, they have forgotten everything the coach went over in pre-game. What have I done? I have established that if you are going to play me, you are going to have to coach. I've got the advantage. When you line up in this manner, 5 can tip to 4. I want the ball to start the game.

DIAGRAM 12-2.

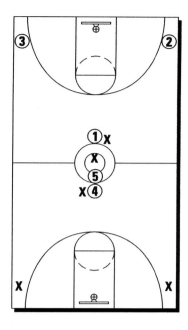

I've got to show you this. Coaches are real smart alecks. They scout. I lined up like this, but my opponent lined up like this. What did this mean? *One of us is going to shoot a layup.*

What do the officials do on the first contact in any game? They blow the whistle. I have a rule. On our first possession of the game, *we are going to drive the ball or post the ball.* Don't shoot the ball outside. The officials are trying to set the tone. I want to go inside because I want to get a foul on their big player. I want to go right at their star because the officials are going to blow the whistle.

What about time-outs? How organized are you in time-outs? Do you tell your players where to sit? What is the procedure when you call a time-out? I want my players to sit in a particular spot on the bench. *We practice time-outs.* We will be running a drill in the first week of practice. You know that some players don't listen to you very well if they aren't in the game.

While you are talking to the five people who are in the game, someone is *looking in the stands* to see if her boyfriend is there. Suddenly, your two post players foul out with two minutes left in the game, and you must put this girl in the game. She hasn't heard one word that you said all night. I've had that happen to me at my level. I cured that. We need a lot of fast-break conditioning drills.

Right in the middle of a drill, I blow the whistle and call time-out. Our players sprint to the sideline, sprint — not jog. Our managers set up chairs on the sideline for five players. My point guard sits to my far right, my center sits to my far left. My 2 guard is in the second seat, my 4 player is next to the center, with 3 in the middle. For the first 15 seconds, my managers give them water, towels, whatever they have to do, get it done. How much time do you get in a one-minute time-out? Forty-five seconds.

I have an assistant whose job depends on us being on the floor when that second horn sounds. Get someone to do it for you. Confer with your assistant if you have one. You have 30 seconds to instruct your players during the time-out. For the first 15 seconds, *make two points.* That's all they are going to remember. The first is why you called the time-out. Then I make one defensive point and one offensive point. I spend the last 15 seconds repeating that. At practice, I designate five players to sit on the chairs. Everyone else gathers around me. We will say, in this drill we want to make four passes before the ball is shot. Secondly, every time the ball is shot, we are going to *box out*. Everybody got that? We start the drill again. We run the drill for about two or three minutes more; we stop again, and my manager passes out note cards to every player. I have them write down the two points that I made during the time-out.

While we are practicing, my managers check the cards. "Coach, two people didn't know what those points were." I take those two people and get two chairs. I put those two people on the chairs right in the center circle. I put the rest of the players on the line, and I have them run drills. Why? Peer pressure. That's what we are in today. If we could motivate with pride like we used to motivate, we would be a lot better off. *Peer pressure is a motivator*. That's the way I end practice. I will guarantee you that tomorrow they will know what I said. What am I trying to do? My players are conditioned to listen during time-outs. They are made to listen. Players will do what they are made to do. You must coach.

Pre-practice routine. Before practice starts they come on the floor, stretch out, shoot *free-throws. Organize your time*. Ever have a player in a bad mood? Are you ever in a bad mood? Ten minutes prior to practice, we have a routine. It includes a little stretching, but we warm up before we stretch. We do ballhandling, etc. I have this set up at six different baskets because during this time, I walk around and I talk to the kids. I want them to see me; I want to see them. I look them in the eye. "How was your day?" Before I start ranting and raving, I want them to see me as a person, and I want them to be a person. You'll know their mood before practice starts. It's a great way to ease the tension, both theirs and mine.

I am going to use numbers here for clarity, but I don't number players any more. We only have point guards, wings and posts on my team. I want to be able to play the five best players. I don't want to get stuck putting someone in the game because a better player wasn't that number. It helps at practice. If your star player is a "2," all other 2's know they aren't going to play. But if she is a wing, then there is also another wing position. It helps.

DIAGRAM 12-3. THE THREE-POINT SHOT

1 dribbles in, and 5 steps out hard. 1 passes to 5 and screens for 3, who stepped the defense into the middle.

DIAGRAM 12-4.

1 goes weakside. 5 passes to 3. 4 ducks in and comes off the screen of 2. 5 also screens, so it is a staggered-screen. We get the defense to the highside then we flatten out. 3 passes to 4 for the shot.

DIAGRAM 12-5.

3 can also drive into the middle and pass back to 1, who has the entire side of the floor. We have two opportunities to shoot the three, 4 or 1.

DIAGRAM 12-6. "TWO DOWN"

1 dribbles away from the double post. 2 back-screens for 3 and goes to the block. 4 and 5 screen down for 2.

DIAGRAM 12-7. CONTINUATION

1 has made the pass back to 2, who came to the top of the circle. 4 and 5 now set the staggered-screen for 3, who breaks to the corner. 4 screens first, then 5. You can do this with a double-screen or a staggered-screen.

DIAGRAM 12-8.

Set it up the same way, except 1 passes to 3 after 3 makes the V-cut.

DIAGRAM 12-9.

1 makes a hard cut and goes wide. 4 and 5 set a screen for 2. Where will the defense be on 2? Highside. You might get that shot.

DIAGRAM 12-10.

If you don't get that shot, 2 has the ball at the top, 1 comes out hard, and if the *reversal pass is denied*, dive to the basket.

DIAGRAM 12-11.

If the ball is reversed from 2 to 1, 3 comes off of the double. 4 then breaks high, and 5 goes low. The top person goes first.

DIAGRAM 12-12.

This gets you back into the 3 out, 2 in set.

There are thousands of plays; how many can your kids remember? You must be able to give the same look, different options. Do you practice the basketball pass in practice? I do. Passing is the lost art of basketball. It's the worst thing we do in basketball. The best players that you had in high school couldn't pass the ball because somebody was always passing it to them, with the possible exception of the point guard. Teach passing. Teach the wrap around pass, the bounce pass, pass and catch on the move.

DIAGRAM 12-13. A PASSING DRILL

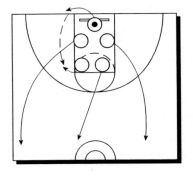

Pass ahead, no rules. 5/0. We run the floor, and the ball cannot touch the floor. Shoot the layup at the other end. Someone takes it out of the net, and we go the other way. Run the lanes. If they drop the ball, they run. This is a good drill for *communication*. "I have the ball, I have left lane, etc."

DIAGRAM 12-14. 3 MAN, 2 BALL DRILL

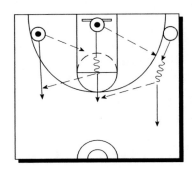

The ball is always passed to the middle man, no skip passes. No play is worth a damn if you can't pass and catch.

DIAGRAM 12-15. LENGTH OF THE FLOOR IN FIVE SECONDS.

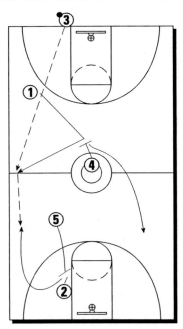

You can make three passes in five seconds. 3 inbounds the ball. 4 acts as if she is going to set a screen for 1. 1 goes hard for the screen, reverse pivots and cuts to the sideline. 5 screens down for 2, who breaks to the sideline. 3 throws the ball at the sideline near mid-court. We tell 3 to throw long, over her head. If 3 overthrows, 2 will get it. 4 goes long on the opposite side. In that situation, all you want is a shot at the basket. If 1 catches the ball, she can pass to 2 or pass to the weakside or dribble drive, but nobody really knows. What you want is to be able to get a shot.

Here's a free-throw game I really like. We shot 73% from the line this year and we don't have great shooters. We were fourth in the country. This game is responsible. Put 2 or 3 at a basket. *Put time on the clock.* We do it for five minutes. We play to 21. The shooter gets a one and one. If she makes the first shot, you now have 20, down from 21. If she misses the second, you are back to 21. If she missed the first one, you add two points, you now have 23. You don't get to shoot the second shot.

The next player in line shoots. The first team to zero wins, or you can play until time runs out and someone may be minus six. The second part of this game is each player has a *sign on them*, it hangs by a string, and it has their free-throw percentage on it. We pair up the best with the worst, etc. We do this drill every day. If you have trouble getting your players to concentrate on free throws, use this drill. Put pressure on them.

Do you know what your team shoots from the line the last five minutes of the game? That's what they really shoot, because that's *pressure.* If you are way ahead and your scrubs are in, it will even out. Know what your shooting percentage is during the last five minutes. The blowouts will balance out the close games. We shot 73% for the season but 66% for the last five minutes of the games.

DIAGRAM 12-16. BOXING OUT ON A FREE-THROW

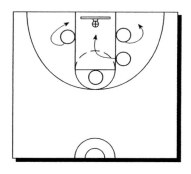

How do you cover the crosses, etc.? We run them. Here is "Inside." The two players on the baseline spin out, and the other goes to the middle.

DIAGRAM 12-17.

When I face a team that is a very good offensive rebounding team, I do this. I put two of my players at half-court. So, they will put two players back. Get them off the lane. That's the player who is killing us on those crossing moves.

DIAGRAM 12-18.

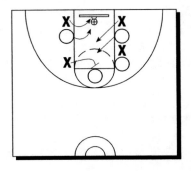

Wherever they go, take them person-to-person. If you are next to me on the lane, you are mine. *Rebounding wins games.* The first stat I look at is offensive rebounds. You can rebound without great players. You must teach them to box out. Do your players know where most of the rebounds go? You must drill that, rebounding to a spot.

CHAPTER 13

SPECIAL SITUATIONS

DANNY SINGLETON

When do you call timeout? Here is what we do.

- Out of control.
- Change of momentum.
- Down early.
- Last second shot.

Conditions of play serve as a traffic light.

"Red-White-Blue" to save a timeout. Can you change a game without a timeout? We feel we can.

RED—DANGER.

We must increase the tempo. We are in serious trouble. On offense we say "OK" with three fingers up. This means it is OK to shoot a "3". "Power" means we're shooting a 2. Power inside—we want it to go inside. We absolutely must know the time and score.

WHITE—NORMAL STYLE OF PLAY

Roar and Dawg... Rebound outlet and run.

Defense and Aggression wins games.

BLUE—EVERYTHING IS BLUE SKIES.

The good guys are in control of the game. We win if the following things happen:

OFFENSE	DEFENSE
No timeouts	No fouls
Great shots or no shots	No OK's
Be deliberate	One FG attempt – the worst thing that can happen.

TEAM GUIDELINES FOR TEAM SUCCESS:

- Keep the coach informed of problems before the fact.
- Know alignments and responsibilities.
- Game face—don't speak to officials or opponents.
- Loose balls belong to our team.
- Speak positively to one another at all times.
- Talk to each other during the game.
- Always be on time.
- Manage your time and don't compromise academics.

DEFENSE:

- Dawg-um ... defensive aggression wins games.
- Contain dribbles.
- Help and recover or rotate.
- FETCH—Don't do anything on rebounding (block out, jump, screen) just fetch.
- Contest all shots.
- Never foul on perimeter jump shots.
- Never foul in trap.
- Double the low post.
- Take out the best perimeter.
- Transition defense or chase for the tip.
- Body flash cutter.
- Be fleet—floored feet. Challenge—but don't leave your feet.

OFFENSE:

- ROAR
- Face-diagonal and down.
- Be a threat to score.
- Fake the make—whatever you are doing fake something else.
- Don't dodge fouls—get to the foul line.
- High percentage shots each possession.
- FETCH
- One point per possession.
- 50% field goals—70% free throws.
- Read the low post defense.
- On 3 be at 23."

- If not a 3-point shooter, straddle the 3-point line, you must be guarded.

ARE YOU A BAD SHOOTER OR A GOOD SHOOTER TAKING BAD SHOTS?

SHOT SELECTION PRIORITY—IN ORDER:

- ROAR.
- Power.
- Hot hand.
- My shot.

Terminology—Offense—1-digit number and call

Defense—2-digit number

Condition—Color

Signals: Circle, Over, Flip, Hank, Loop, Hack, Sideline, Cross, Rover, Power, Flood, Deny, Baseline, Wide, Shuffle, Bump, OK, 1, Hi, Lo.

RANK YOUR PLAYERS: WHO STARTS FOR YOU?

- 1-2-3-4-5

WHO ARE YOUR FIRST SUBS?

- Perimeter (6)
- Post (7)

WHO ARE THE NEXT THREE RESERVE PLAYERS?

- 8-9-10

Make this list:

- After the end of the past season.
- Before summer.
- After summer.
- Before the first practice.

POST DRILL—KEEP FIVE OR SIX POST PLAYERS.

X merges with dummy—Hit players between shoulders and mid-back. Two balls at the same time. P—post flash across to low post for entry.

- Score—Rebound—outlet pass
- Switch lines

Switch—go baseline side to topside. Play inside while the other plays outside.

Emphasis:

- Score
- Ball doesn't touch the floor
- Dropstep

CHAPTER 14

LAST SECOND SITUATIONS

JERRY WAINWRIGHT

There is a game within a game. It includes:

- The first possession of every quarter.
- All out-of-bound plays, endline and sideline.
- Every play after a time out.

Over the last 14 years, I have charted every game for the game within a game. For example, if we score on an out-of-bounds play, we get a point. If we are stopped from scoring, the other team gets a point. The correlation of winning the game within a game, and the game itself is over 90%. As a coach, you can control this because some things are consistent. There is a stoppage of play. You can set your defense and set your offense. We spend from 5-to-7 minutes in practice on special situations at the beginning of practice, always 5/0. I do it early because it indicates that it is important. At the end of practice, we do special situations live. If we really do our jobs as coaches, kids will never see anything in a game that they haven't seen in practice. In these late situations, you need a "go to" player.

DIAGRAM 14-1.

You can run this against man or zone and you can run it out of a lot of sets. 1 passes to 4 and cuts to the ballside block. 2 goes to the other block. 3 V-cuts and comes to the perimeter and gets the pass from 4.

DIAGRAM 14-2.

The big players now screen down for 1 and 2.

DIAGRAM 14-3.

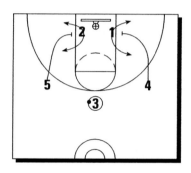

If the defense is playing zone, we would run the same thing except we would screen the bottom of the zone.

DIAGRAM 14-4.

You can also run it from the stack. It ends up the same, 4 and 5 out, 2 and 1 on the block. 1 passes to 4, who passes to 3.

DIAGRAM 14-5.

1 and 2 can now back-screen. Or, we can down-screen on one side and back-screen on the other. This is a good catch-all play for late in the game because you don't know what the defense will be.

Full court situation. At the beginning of the season, we put players on the endline and they have three seconds to go the length of the floor and shoot. We time them. They will always shoot too soon. Most players don't have a good clock in their head. You need to show them that. This has really helped us. You know that often a player is dribbling with momentum and he pulls the trigger way too soon. You should have a primary inbounder and you should find out who can throw the ball full court the best. Have them throw at least seven and always throw to a target, not to a player. Practice this. When a team scores against you late in the game, they will immediately relax. Practice taking the ball out-of-bounds and immediately throwing it down court to a target. We have a designated "fly man." Don't look for that man, throw to the target. The man will be there.

DIAGRAM 14-6.

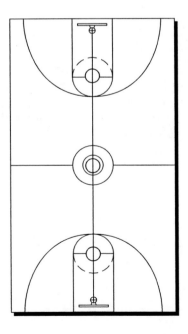

There are two kinds of alignments that bother people. One is the direct line. There is no helpside, there is no ballside. You are forced to pick a side. The most difficult throw to defend is the one right over your head.

DIAGRAM 14-7.

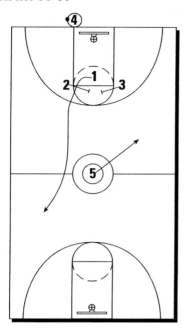

This alignment bothers people. I saw a team have 2 and 3 pinch and 1 broke long and if you get the ball into the front court you can always call time out. The best out-of-bounds plays are run from half-court. There are two decisions you must make. Are you going to run a full-court play or are you going to get to half-court and call time out? The next decision is this. Are we going to call time out when we have a chance to win the game? That's a hard one. I have always felt better not calling time out because we practice this way. But, your kids must know that and they must practice it. They must get right into what you are going to do. Also, are you going to foul if you are up three? I change this game to game. It will depend on who we are playing. If you haven't made up your mind beforehand, there will be indecision. If it doesn't work out, you will lose your kids' trust.

DIAGRAM 14-8.

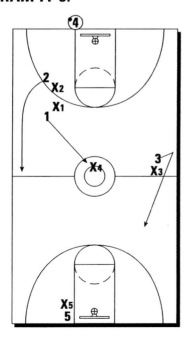

I've had a lot of luck with this alignment. 3 is my best player. If you know the defense isn't going to have someone on the ball, then you need to draw people closer to the endline. Usually X4 will float near mid-court. It is hard to guard 1 and 2 if they line up like this. Always take one of these players and run him directly at the floater, X4. You can eliminate the center fielder with a cutter.

DIAGRAM 14-9.

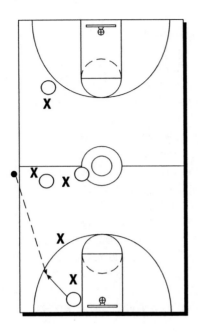

It's amazing how many times you can make this pass.

DIAGRAM 14-10.

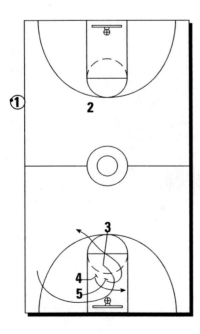

Here is a play we used. If you put all five of your players ballside on a sideline out of bounds, all the defenders will be on the ballside. 4 and 5 double-screen for 3. 5 then comes off of 4 and 4 breaks low.

DIAGRAM 14-11.

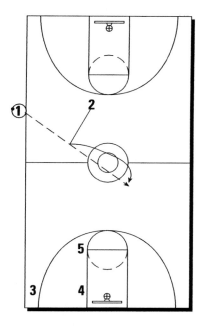

We have 3, a shooter, in the corner. 4 is at the rim. 2 will break to the ball and then away and there is no one on that side of the floor to defend 2. But we set that up by putting everyone on ballside.

DIAGRAM 14-12.

I bet I have about one hundred plays for three-point shots late in the game. This is a very simple one. Almost every coach in America says "Give up two" and they are guarding the perimeter. I say that human nature says that any pass you make to the inside, someone will turn their head. They have been conditioned to get to the level of the ball. If the perimeter man will move opposite of the turn of the head and get the return pass from inside, it will get you a better shot than any play you have ever drawn. We work on it every day. Practice this as a shooting drill.

Let me finish by telling you, don't give up. Don't give in. Continue to do what you have been doing. The only way to be successful is to do it your way and do it consistently. All the discipline, all the rules must be administered fairly. Please don't believe coaches must give in to what the principles of coaching are. They are the same as the principles of teaching. You will give them something they can't get anywhere else so they can progressively become successful and, most of all, a happy adult.

CHAPTER 15

SPECIAL SITUATIONS: IDEAS, CONCEPTS AND PLAYS

JERRY WAINWRIGHT

LATE-GAME SITUATIONS — THOUGHTS:

- One of the most important parts of the game, yet one of the most overlooked.
- Majority of games are won and lost by eight or fewer points (three or four possessions)
- Defense, offense, shooting, etc., is taught by repetition—do the same with late-game situations (every day).
- Must be more than just a segment of practice; coach it just like it's a game, i.e., from the bench, calling TOs, substituting, etc.
- Each member of the team must know time, score, and situation.
- Must work on all possibilities—up big, up a little, tied, down big, down a little, different time left (five minutes on down), different foul situations, different personnel.
- Theory is "you've experienced it before, you know what needs to be done."
- Occasionally make bad calls (even fouling out players), maybe even taunting to get player's reactions. Call T's.
- Substitutions to stop clock or "O"/"D."
- Know best player to go to, best play to call, best "D" to use (maybe different at home and on the road).
- Have a philosophy—make sure everyone knows and understands it.
- Know what you want to do, but have a contingency plan.
- Should never face anything in a game your players haven't experienced.

LATE-GAME SITUATIONS — QUESTIONS TO ASK:

- If behind, do you want to foul or go for steal/TO?
  If foul, whom and when?
- If up three, do you foul to avoid three-pointer? If so, when?
- If down one, two, or tied, do you want to hold for last shot or take first good one?
- After getting rebound/TO (or after made shot), do you want to immediately call time, push it up and call time, disregard time out and go for score?
- Do you like "two for one", i.e., shoot so the opponent gets the ball with more than 45 seconds, so you can get it back?
- Do you have plays from all locations (taking time left into account)?

IDEAS — LAST-SECOND SITUATIONS:

Practice situations:

- Use clock and officials.
- Varsity vs. JVs with varsity 10 points down.
- Big people vs. little people—build role appreciation.
- Drill running actions where players have one second to shoot.
- Call team together in practice, give them situation and play, then test them on it. Also do in classroom.

END-OF-GAME PHILOSOPHY:

- Delay game:
  ✓ Keep clock running; take sure shot; open up the floor.
- Freeze game:
  ✓ No shots unless a layup (uncontested) or free throw.
  ✓ Use when you have enough points to win or you want the last shot.

OVERLOAD SCRIMMAGE SITUATIONS:

- Using six defensive players while perfecting the half-court trap press offense.
- Using seven defensive players when advancing the ball up against a three-quarter-court zone press.
- Using eight defensive players when operating the full-court press offense.
- Using six offensive players to strengthen the zone defense.

REASONS FOR A COACH TO CALL A TIMEOUT IN THE LAST MINUTE:

- To calm the players.
- To reinforce and motivate the players.
- To run a special play or to cover a special situation.
- To cover individual assignments.
- To break the opponent's momentum.
- To settle down the crowd.
- To make an opposing free-throw shooter think about the shot.
- To give the players a rest.
- To stop the clock.
- To make a defensive change.

GAME SITUATIONS TO PRACTICE:

One-Point Series:

Five seconds are put on the clock and the situations practiced are:

- A one-point lead and the ball in the process of shooting a one-one.
- A one-point lead with the ball out of bounds from the sideline.
- A one-point lead with the ball out of bounds at the end line.
- A one-point lead with the ball out of bounds under the offensive basket.
- A one-point lead without the ball—sideline out of bounds.
- A one-point lead without the ball—end line out of bounds.

Two-Point Series:

The two-point series operates under the same situation outlined above, except the point spread is two with 10 seconds remaining.

Three-Point Series:

The three-point series follows the same pattern with a three-point spread and 20 seconds remaining.

Four-Point Series:

The four-point series involves a four-point spread with 30 seconds remaining.

GAME SITUATIONS TO PRACTICE:

- One minute to go, score tied, your team has the ball
- One minute to go, score tied, your team is on defense
- One minute to go, trailing by one, two, or three points, your ball under opponent's basket
- One minute to go, ahead by one, two, or three points
- One minute to go, behind by four or five points, with opponent having the ball
- Ten seconds to go, opponent has just scored the go-ahead points
- Ten seconds to go, score tied, you have the ball in back court
- Ten seconds to go, trail by two or three points, opponent has the ball
- Two seconds to go, lead by one, two, or three points, opponent has the ball
- Two seconds to go, lead by one, two, or three points, opponent has ball out of bounds under your basket

SPECIAL OFFENSE — ALL-PURPOSE ACTION

DIAGRAM 15-1.

Players align in 1-4 set (with post players on wing). 1 passes to 5 and cuts through the lane to the ballside box. 2 slices across the lane to the opposite box. 3 steps down lane to dotted line and then V-cuts to the high post.

DIAGRAM 15-2.

5 passes to 3, steps to the ball and then down-screens for 1. 4 steps to the ball, then down-screens for 2. 5 and 4 open to the ball after screening. 3 makes a play for himself or hits the open man.

Note:

- Can run this action against zone defense also. Just screen zone areas and cutters flare.
- Can run this action from different sets, just to the post man, who breaks out.
- Can use as a last-second play or as shot clock runs down.

SPECIAL SITUATIONS — 7-TO-12 SECOND PLAY

DIAGRAM 15-3.

1 dribbles 2 down. 4 screens across for 3 and then receives a screen from 5. 3 continues across off screen down by 2. 1 passes to open man.

MAN-TO-MAN ACTION — DOUBLE-SINGLE READ

DIAGRAM 15-4.

3 is screener. 5 and 3 move across the lane to set a double-screen for 2. 4 cuts off 5 to opposite block. 2 cuts off double-screen, then off the single-screen by 5.

DIAGRAM 15-5.

If 2 reads that the defense is cheating on the double, he pops back to the wing.

MAN-TO-MAN ACTION — SCREEN FOR SCREENER

DIAGRAM 15-6.

5 is the scorer. 5 sets a screen for 2. 2 continues off the second screen for 3. 4 screens down for 5, who pops to the wing for the jumper.

OUT OF BOUNDS — SIDE — PITTSBURGH ACTION

DIAGRAM 15-7.

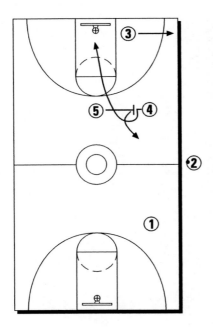

Players align as shown. 5 back-screens for 4, who rolls off screen to the basket, looking for the lob. 5, after the screen, comes to the ball. 3 reads the defense, and either holds post, or cuts to the corner. (He is a one-on-one option). 1 holds in backcourt if no one plays him for the "safe" in.

DIAGRAM 15-8.

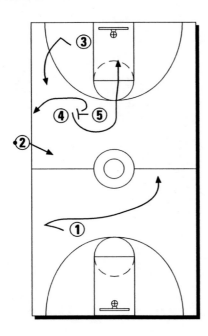

If the defense plays 1 hard, he walks him to the ball, then cuts hard backside where there is no help. After inbounding, 2 steps into open area.

Note: If 1 receives ball in backcourt, get right into offense.

OUT OF BOUNDS — SIDE "A" PLAY

DIAGRAM 15-9.

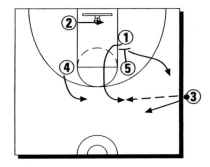

Players align in box. 2 is the primary shooter. 5 down-screens for 1, then opens and cuts to the ball. 1 cuts to the top of the circle and receives the inbound pass. 3 steps in. 2 puts "head" under basket.

DIAGRAM 15-10.

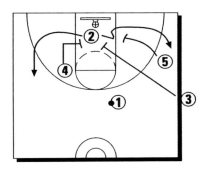

5 and 3 double down-screen for 2. 4 down-screens for 2. 2 comes off screens to either side.

Note: Use versus man or zone defense.

OUT OF BOUNDS — SIDE "B" PLAY

DIAGRAM 15-11.

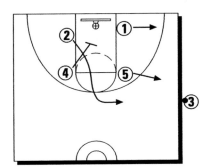

Players align in box set, 2 and 4 good shooters. On ball slap, 1 and 5 cut to the ballside, 4 down-screens for 2.

DIAGRAM 15-12.

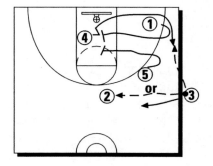

1 and 5 step back to double-screen for 2. 3 inbounds to 2 or 4, then steps in.

DIAGRAM 15-13.

If time permits a second pass, return the ball to 3 on a step-in.

Note: Use versus man or zone defense. Good play when you need to score on first pass.

OUT OF BOUNDS — SIDE — PENN ACTION

DIAGRAM 15-14.

Players align as shown; 2 inbounds the ball. 1 frees himself and receives inbound pass. 4 V-cuts to wing. 2 steps in after inbounding the ball and shuffle cuts off the double-screen set by 3 and 5 to opposite box. 1 looks to pass directly to 2.

DIAGRAM 15-15.

If the pass to 2 is not open, 3 steps out and receives pass from 1. 1 shuffle-cuts off 5 to ball side box.

DIAGRAM 15-16.

3 reverses ball to 5, who steps out after setting a shuffle-cut screen. 3 and 4 down-screen for 1 and 2 and then roll back. 5 passes the to open man.

OUT OF BOUNDS — SIDE — IVY

DIAGRAM 15-17.

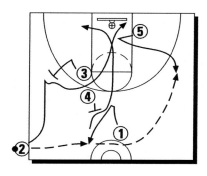

1 V-cuts to free himself and gets the inbound pass from 2. 5 breaks out and receives the pass from 1. 1 cuts off 4's back-screen and goes to the box. 2 steps in and V-cuts off 3's backside to the ballside box. 4 steps out after setting a back-screen.

DIAGRAM 15-18.

5 passes to 4, steps to the ball, and down-screens for 2. 3 opens and down-screens for 1. 3 and 5 open after down-screening. 4 passes to the open man.

OUT OF BOUNDS

Side: Versus Pressure Man-to-Man defense

Action: Versus Man on the Ball

DIAGRAM 15-19.

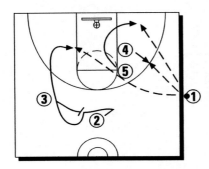

4 breaks to the ball. 5 rolls down and posts. 3 back-screens for 2. 2 steps to the ball, then cuts off the back-screen, looking for the lob. 1 inbounds to the open man.

DIAGRAM 15-20.

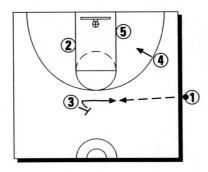

3 rolls back to the ball after setting a back-screen as the outlet.

OUT OF BOUNDS — SIDE — POST-FEED ACTION

DIAGRAM 15-21.

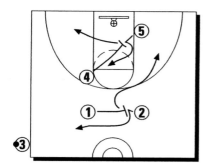

1 screens for 2, then fades. 4 diagonally down-screens for 5 and rolls hard to corner. 5 cuts hard off the down-screen to "L."

DIAGRAM 15-22.

3 inbounds to 4. 5 rolls hard down the lane, looking for the ball.

OUT OF BOUNDS — SIDE — DIRECT PASS (LAST SECONDS)

DIAGRAM 15-23.

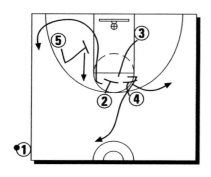

Players align as shown. 1 is inbounder. On signal from inbounder, 2 and 4 double-screen down for 3. After setting the double-screen, 2 continues to the corner off the screen by 5. 5 steps up the lane after setting the screen. After setting the double-screen, 4 spots up to the wing. 3 comes off the double-screen ready to shoot. 1 passes to the open man.

OUT OF BOUNDS — SIDE — LAST-SECOND SHOT

DIAGRAM 15-24.

1 back-screens for 2, who cuts to the basket, looking for the lob. 1 comes to the ball after setting a back-screen. 3 cuts off 5's screen to the ball. 5 opens after the screen. 4 steps in after entering the ball for a return pass and three-point shot.

OUT OF BOUNDS — SIDE — ACTION FOR UNDER SEVEN SECONDS

DIAGRAM 15-25.

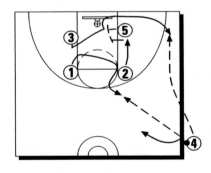

Players align in box set. 2 moves down toward 5. 2 holds in double-screen with 5. 3 fakes up and cuts off double. 1 flashes to the ballside elbow. 4 steps in for return pass.

OUT OF BOUNDS — SIDE — LAST SECONDS — CELTICS ACTION

DIAGRAM 15-26.

2 takes two steps to down-screen for the shooter (5). 5 cuts hard to the level of the screen, then fades to corner, looking for the lob pass from 1. 4 down-screens for 3, who comes hard to the ball. 4 then opens to the basket.

OUT OF BOUNDS—SIDE—LAST- SECONDS ACTION

DIAGRAM 15-27.

2 and 3 line up side by side. On slap of the ball, 3 cuts over 2. As he passes him, 2 flashes to sideline. 4 screens down for 3 and then rolls to basket. 1 steps to the ball and fades.

SIDELINE OUT OF BOUNDS—MILWAUKEE (LAST-SECOND PLAY FOR THREE POINTS)

DIAGRAM 15-28.

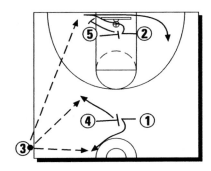

Players align in box as shown with 3 inbounding ball. On signal, 4 screens for 1 and rolls back. 1 breaks to the ball. 5 screens across for 2. 2 breaks out off 5's screen, then backcuts off 5's back-screen. 3 inbounds to 1, 4, or if open, 2 on his first cut.

DIAGRAM 15-29.

If inbounded to 1, and 2 is not open, he penetrates. 3 steps in and comes off a back-screen by 5 to the box.

DIAGRAM 15-30.

3 then breaks off the double-screen by 5 and 4 to the three-point range. 4 wheels off of 5 to three-point range and 5 opens in the lane. 2 fades. 1 hits the open man.

SPECIAL 3/4 COURT — ACTION — DOUBLE-SCREEN FOR SHOOTER — LAST SECONDS (TENNESSEE ACTION)

DIAGRAM 15-31.

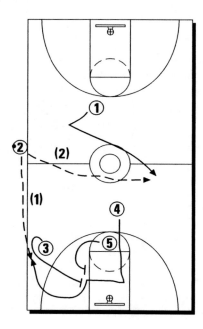

4 is the best shooter. 4 cuts away, then comes off a double by 5 and 3. 1 steps to the ball, then cuts backside. 2 looks to 4, then to 1.

SPECIAL 3/4 COURT — ACTION — LAST SECONDS

DIAGRAM 15-32.

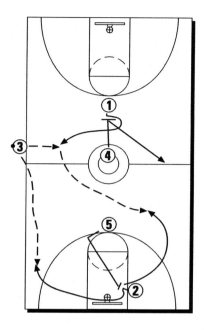

4 screens for 1. 1 cuts up the sideline to the ball. 4 fades opposite. 5 screens for 2 and rolls back. 2 cuts off the screen toward the ball. 3 passes to the open man.

SPECIAL 3/4 COURT — ACTION — DEEP FOR LAYUP

DIAGRAM 15-33.

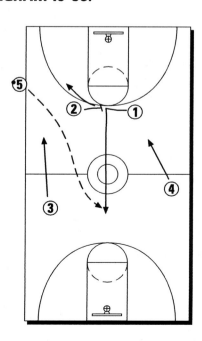

3 and 4 break hard to the ball. 2 pivots to set a screen for 1 and then rolls back. 1 cuts hard to the level of the screen and then streaks deep.

SPECIAL FULL COURT — ACTION — TO CALL TIMEOUT AT HALF COURT

DIAGRAM 15-34.

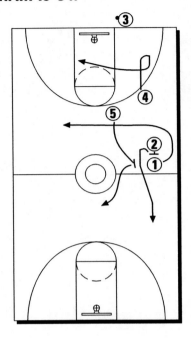

4 steps to the ball, reverses pivot and cuts across the lane. 2 and 5 screen for 1, then break deep. 1 curls off the double-screen, breaking hard to the sideline.

DIAGRAM 15-35.

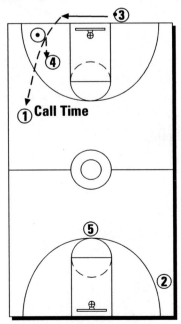

3 inbounds to 4. 4 looks up the sideline to pass to 1. 1 catches the pass and immediately calls time.

SPECIAL FULL COURT — LAST SECONDS
Three-Point Action

DIAGRAM 15-36.

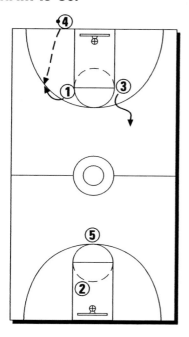

5 is the best screener, 2 the best shooter. 4 inbounds to 1. 3 flares.

DIAGRAM 15-37.

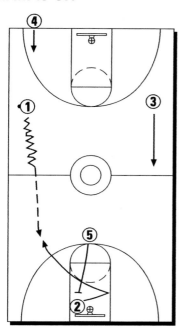

1 "pushes" the ball. 5 down-screens for 2. 3 flares wide. 1 looks to pass to 2 for the shot.

SPECIAL FULL COURT — ACTION — LAST SECONDS

DIAGRAM 15-38.

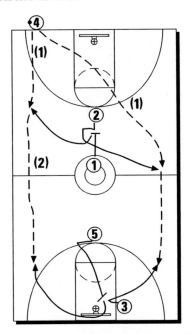

1 screens for 2 and then cuts opposite 2's cut. 5 screens for 3 and then rolls opposite 3's cut. 4 passes to the open man.

SPECIAL SITUATIONS—NO TIMEOUTS LEFT
(Five Seconds or Less)

DIAGRAM 15-39.

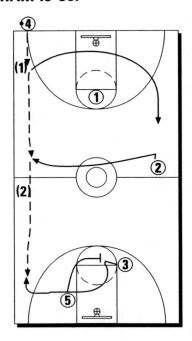

1 fakes hard and comes to the ball, then empties on the back-side wing. 2 fakes to the ball, then cuts hard across the court. 4 tries to inbound the ball to 2 on the move. When 2 receives the ball, 5 "head hunts" on a screen for 3. 3 sets his man up and curls off the screen by 5.

DIAGRAM 15-40.

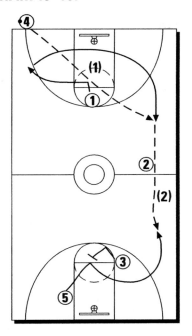

If the ball is inbounded to 1, 3 screens for 5.

SPECIAL FULL COURT — ACTION — UNDER FIVE SECONDS

DIAGRAM 15-41.

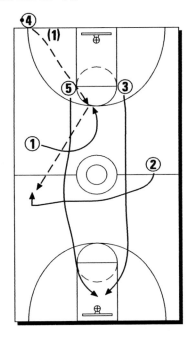

1 is the best passer and 2 is the best shooter. 5 and 3 sprint deep to rebound. 1 circles through center and tries to get the inbound pass at top of circle. 2 delays a count, then sprints opposite at a diagonal. 1 looks to 2. If he is not open, he dribbles for shot.

SPECIAL FULL COURT — ACTION VS. MAN-TO-MAN DEFENSE

DIAGRAM 15-42.

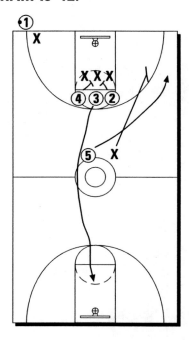

Against man on the ball defense: 5 breaks to the ball. 2 and 4 pinch in to screen and 3 cuts deep.

DIAGRAM 15-43.

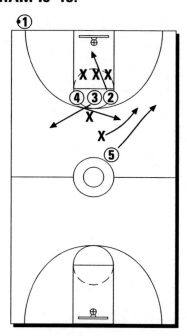

Against man off the ball defense: 5 breaks to the ball. 4 and 3 x-cut as 2 breaks to the ball.

SPECIAL FULL COURT — ACTION — DOUBLE STACK VS. MAN OFF THE BALL

DIAGRAM 15-44.

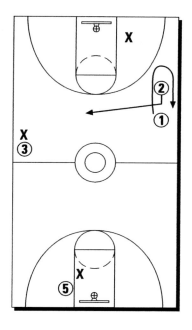

1 is the best ball handler, 3 is the best player. 1 cuts around 2, 2 then cuts diagonally. 3 reads the defense. 5 holds deep. Anytime 2 gets the inbound pass, 1 cuts back to the ball.

DIAGRAM 15-45.

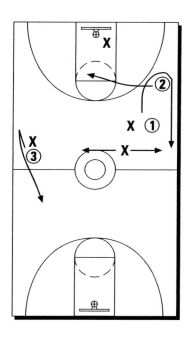

4 reads the defensive man off the ball.

FULL COURT SPECIAL — "HOME RUN" ACTION
(Last-Seconds Play)

DIAGRAM 15-46.

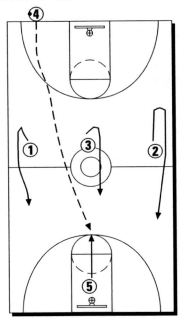

Players align as shown. 5 breaks from under the basket up the lane to receive the pass from 4. If possible, 5 catches and shoots immediately. If 5 can't make the catch, he "taps" the ball to one of the three men filling the lanes.

Note: Use with two seconds or less.

FULL COURT SPECIAL — "HOME RUN" — BALL-SCREEN COUNTER
(Last-Seconds Play)

DIAGRAM 15-47.

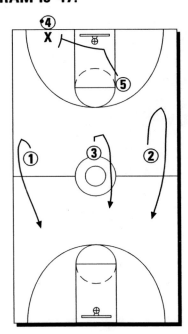

Players align as shown. 1, 3, and 2 step hard to the ball and then break deep. 4 fakes pass and then runs baseline. 5 attempts to "blind pick" the man on the ball.

Note: Tell the referee what you are going to do. 5 must take the "hit." Use with two seconds or less to go. Use only when you can run the baseline. Use when the defense has a man aggressively on the ball. Use when you have a timeout left, so if it doesn't work, you can call it.

CHAPTER 16

TEACHING THE "3"

ROY WILLIAMS

The two best things Coach Dean Smith told me during the 10 years I worked with him at North Carolina were: 1) *be yourself*, and 2) don't be stuck with *one style or philosophy*. Make your style and philosophy fit your players. We change each year. We use some plays every year, but change the position of the players.

DIAGRAM 16-1.

Here is a good out-of-bounds play. 3 has the ball out-of-bounds. 4 and 5 double-screen for 2, who is our best player. Against a man-to-man, X4 and X5 are on the inside. The only way 2 can be covered is that X5 can switch out to 2. We tell 2 to read X2, get him low enough to *rub off on the screen.*

DIAGRAM 16-2.

They may switch, but if they do, 1 steps hard to the ball and 1 sets a screen for 5 who comes down the lane. If they switched with X2 and X5, you have a smaller person guarding 5.

You must understand my *philosophy on the three-point shot.* In my first five years at Kansas, 51.5% was the lowest field goal percentage we had. In that five-year period, we were first out of 298 Division I teams. This past year we were 47.2% which is a heck of a drop. That was the lowest. In 1990, we were 53.5% and led the nation in field goal percentage and shot more three-pointers in the Big Eight than any other team. Three of our kids had the green light to shoot the three. They could shoot the "3" any time as long as there was more than one defensive player back. This year we shot 47.2% and that's not good.

We had to *find a way* to win games. In the past, we *outscored* people. This year the other team had three defensive people in the lane because we could not shoot as well. We had less than five *backdoor layups* for the entire season. We had fewer *drives* to the basket than we ever had and that's because three players were not guarded when they went outside of the three-point line. That made it difficult for us to score a lot of points, especially with the elimination of the five-second dribbling rule. That took away our pressure on the wings. We didn't get as many steals, therefore, we didn't get as much scoring from our defense.

We decided we were going to win this year with the *defensive field goal percentage,* and our *rebounding.* We were 7th out of 298 with defensive field goal percentage, 38.6%. Your job is to find a way to win.

DIAGRAM 16-3.

This is *against a zone* to get a three-point shot. 3 takes it out. Every play we have is designed to get a layup with an option for the three-point shot. We wanted the ball to go inside first. It is a *high-percentage shot* and at the end of the game, we don't want to be playing against your five best players. By taking the ball inside first, I have a chance to get you in foul trouble and by the end of the game, one or two of your best players may be fouled out.

This is called "#2." 4 sets a screen for 5. 5 comes down the lane. We will always take the *layup* if he is open, but if he isn't, he goes to the corner. 4, after the screen, will roll into the lane. 1 will screen for 2.

DIAGRAM 16-4.

3 passes to 5, and steps in. 5 can pass to 3. Here 5 passes to 2 as 4 moves into the high post. 2 passes to 1. 4 must come across below the foul line, right about where the old dotted line was. We want 4 to occupy X4. 3 screens for 5 to go behind for the lob. You don't need anyone who can dunk. 5 can go up, catch the ball, then power the ball back up. It may be better because 5 has a better chance of being fouled.

DIAGRAM 16-5.

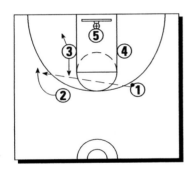

When that happens, 3 steps out into this area. Now, I am going to decide which man to screen because we are sending 2 behind that screen for the cross-court pass from 1. 2 has a three-point shot. 3 screens either the *top or bottom man* of that zone, whoever comes out. So, the ball went from 3-5-2-1-2.

DIAGRAM 16-6.

Against a Man Defense. *"Double."* 2 takes it out. 3 either comes around or has 4 and 5 set the double-screen. 4 then screens again for 5. 1 fakes inside and then steps wide.

DIAGRAM 16-7.

3 is near the corner; 5 is on the perimeter; 4 at the top of the key. The ball goes from 2-3-5-4. 4 fakes hard to 1 because we want the defense to shift. 3 and 5 set a double-screen, and 2 comes off for the three-point shot.

DIAGRAM 16-8.

Against a zone, we *cross-screen*. 3 screens high; 5 screens low, and 2 comes off for the shot. The cross-screen gives us a better angle.

DIAGRAM 16-9.

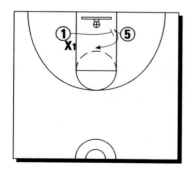

1 is in the low-post area, and 1 screens for 5; 2 lobs to 5. You can use *"double"* against a zone or man.

DIAGRAM 16-10. "PENETRATION"

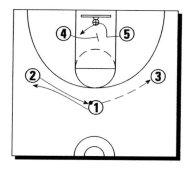

1 can pass to either side, usually away from your best shooter. 1 passes to 3, and there is a quick exchange between 1 and 2. When 3 catches the ball, he kills a little time to wait for 2 to get to the top of the key. 3 penetrates toward the middle, not the baseline. 4 screens anyone in the middle of the zone. Or, if there is not a middle man, 4 will screen all the way across the zone. 5 goes behind, curls and looks for the pass from 3. 5 must go to the baseline side and get inside the weakside forward.

DIAGRAM 16-11.

At the same time, 1 comes back and screens for 2 who moves for the three-point shot.

DIAGRAM 16-12.

This is *against a man-to-man*. We put 4 and 5 at the elbows and initiate our offense by hitting either. I don't think 4 or 5 will get out and pressure as much as 2 or 3, so I know we can get our offense started. If 4 and 5 are pressured, 2 and 3 come up. 4 and 5 are interchangeable. They have three ways they can get open. They can *bump, cross,* or 4 can *screen* for 5 and then cross. Let's say that they go at this team, but the other team does not let them get the ball. In that case, 2 and 3 will come up the lane hard. They have the same options; *bump, cross, or screen.*

DIAGRAM 16-13. "POST OPTION"

Let's say we hit 3. 5 goes backdoor. 3's first look is to 5, a two-handed bounce pass. If 5 doesn't get it, he swivels back and gets the defender on his back. 4 is thinking rebound. 2 screens for 1 who goes to the weakside. 3 has the ball.

DIAGRAM 16-14.

3 can pass to 1 for the three-point shot. As soon as 3 passes to 1, 3 sets a screen for 2, who flares for the possible pass from 1. We then have somebody in position to shoot the three-point shot from either side. 4's thought is that one of his teammates is going to shoot and he should get *inside position*. If you ask me, our best shot is the *layup*, and then having the backboard covered when someone shoots. We don't like surprises. I'll stop practice and ask how many liked a shot. Sometimes I do that on a good shot. I want to be sure that everyone understands what is a good shot.

DIAGRAM 16-15. SECONDARY BREAK

The only time we run the *secondary break* is when there are more than two defenders back. If there are two or less, we want a *quick shot* and that should be our *primary break*. If there are more than two, we take the ball to the baseline and *flatten out* the defense. We want to *attack* before you can get to the man you are supposed to be guarding. 3 looks in to 5. 3 passes to 1 who looks in to 5. 1 passes to 4 who looks in to 5 and then reverses the ball to 2. 2 looks into 5 as 5 works across the lane. As 4 passes to 2, 3 moves in and then comes high and sets a backscreen for 4 to go for the lob.

DIAGRAM 16-16.

If 4 didn't get the lob, he continues across and screens for 5 as 2 passes to 3. 5 must go the baseline side and wants to get inside the baseline defense. 4 or 5 is open much of the time. A *teaching point* is that when 3 sets the screen, 3 just turns for the ball. 3 does not go out wider. We want 3 as tight as he can be. We go from this into motion.

DIAGRAM 16-17. "SECONDARY BREAK FOR A 3"

We must call this. This is a good shot near the end of the game. 1 will penetrate and pass out to 3. 4 goes to the block; 5 stops at the top of the key.

DIAGRAM 16-18.

3 will pass to 1 or skip-pass to 5. 5 fakes to 2; 3 comes up and screens for 1, and 5 passes to 1 near the corner.

DIAGRAM 16-19. "REVERSE FOR 3"

Same situation. 3 has the ball who passes to 1 to 5. 5 makes the fake to 2 as 4 comes up the lane. 4 will then turn and set a doublescreen with 1. 3 comes off the doublescreen for the shot. So, the ball goes from 3-1-5-3. This can also be run against the zone.

DIAGRAM 16-20. "ISOLATION"

1 chooses a side, and 5 head hunts on the opposite side. 1 passes back to 3 for the three-point shot. Remember, we are running hard with our biggest player setting the screen.

DIAGRAM 16- 21.

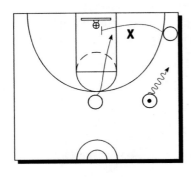

In our secondary break against a zone, the only difference is that the screener for the lob will screen anyone in the middle of the zone from the side. The lob must go inside to anybody in that back zone. I said 3 doesn't come out after setting the backscreen vs the man defense. Against a zone, 3 will have to come out higher. Other than that, they are the same. We want to run the secondary break after a make or a miss so quickly you cannot get set up to guard the man you are supposed to be guarding. Three different times this year the other team scored and four seconds later, we scored at the other end.

Let me give you the free-lance rules that tie in with the secondary break. If we don't get the primary or secondary break, we go into our free-lance offense vs a set defense. We have three rules. 1) 3 passes unless there is a layup. 2) Change sides of the floor. 3) Give the defense a chance to make a mistake. Think about the teams in your league. You know after two passes how strong it is; after four passes it's not quite as strong; after six passes it's not strong at all. Now, if there are two or fewer back vs the break, we are going to try to get a shot in two or fewer passes. We want to get the ball inside and when you change sides of the floor, it kills the pivot defense.